G Force
&
H Bomb

Confessions of a
neurotypical mum

By

Sleepless in Norfolk

ISBN: 1503242498
ISBN-13: 978-1503242494

DEDICATION

This book is dedicated to all the friends and family who have helped us along the way. Be it a spare pair of hands, a place of refuge, a cuppa or a prosecco to share, a listening ear.
I am truly blessed to have you.

You know who you are!

For my dear boys and my long suffering hubby: what would I do without you!

To pinch a phrase from the young one:
"Mummy loves you SO much… Squeezy hug!!"

CONTENTS

Sleepless in Norfolk

ACKNOWLEDGMENTS

Damn, I really NEED to put something on this page as I can't figure out how to remove it without messing up the page numbering. Hmm…

Oh wait!! Only kidding!

I have to acknowledge my truly wonderful personal assistant here for her contributions to my journal.

Also a big thank you to the talented Mia Dunton for designing the cover.

Many thanks too to all of my lovely proof-readers; my "book club" who persuaded me to publish this rather personal account. All the people I've driven mad with questions and requests for feedback: sorry guys!!

This book editing stuff isn't easy you know!

Introducing "G Force" and "H Bomb"
(an affectionate term coined by a friend of mine)

So this is kind of a sample of life in our family; but primarily that of our 2 boys, G and H.

Here's a bit of background.

I'm married to a chap who served in the RAF. I'm going to call him… 'Steve.' I spent the first 8 years of our married life following him from West Norfolk, to Germany, to East Norfolk, then back to Germany. I went out to Germany the second time pregnant with G, having had IVF in the UK.

I guess there were a few teething problems from the start, but nothing that flagged up to us newbie parents any major concerns.

Here's a potted history from G's birth to initial diagnosis.

*   Born by C section at 38 weeks due to there being no fluid left in the womb and the placenta was dying. The fluid was all pretty much spread around my body, interestingly on my feet. It was rather like walking on a layer of jelly, with another layer attached to the top of your feet. It was an interesting experience trying to flex my feet going up and down stairs, really quite odd.

*   G screamed at night. A lot. Typically from early evening up to

around 3am – he just wouldn't settle. They said it was colic, but that didn't seem to fit. I tried everything: white noise, swaddling, (that worked for one night only) music, baths, lavender, etc. We took it in turns to walk around the local village with him, as the pushchair or the car (no stopping at junctions though please!) seemed to be the only thing that helped. Thank heavens we were in Germany and had the autobahn to zip along. I also soon perfected the art of laying him belly down on my forearm and swinging and bouncing him from side to side while standing.

- At 7 weeks old we notice a small lump below his ear, turns out this was a haemangioma. Kind of like a strawberry birthmark below the skin. Because this was very near his parotid gland (which produces saliva) they had to be sure. He had lots of tests in various hospitals and they discovered it was a load of aggressively growing blood vessels, so they couldn't cut it out without bleeding the poor boy out.

- 3-4 months old: more hospital trips and tests, plus 2 trips to see a specialist in Berlin for keyhole laser treatment. The second trip he picked up a severe bout of gastro-enteritis causing him to spend his first Christmas in a 2 week stay in hospital.

- Ok so he's a little late being weaned, but we put this down to the hospital trips putting him back with the nasal feeding that he needed etc.

- He's still crawling at 14 months, but his speed along the floor is truly impressive.

- 18 months: No words yet but you know how it is... everyone has a story of a late talker who is doing just marvellously now.

- 20 months: he used to eat ok I suppose; he liked being spoon fed baked beans, meat pies, mash etc. As soon as he could finger feed himself though he didn't want you to do it, and didn't want to use utensils either. Whatever he could touch without it being too gooey was ok by him. Over the years it got drier and drier.

- 22 months: I need a repeat prescription for G's soya milk. He had a little reflux as a baby and had never taken to regular milk. I am referred to the paediatrician to review G's milk.

- 23 months: I take G to the Paediatrician. G sits in the corner spinning the wheels of toy cars, and turning his hand over and back repeatedly, giggling hysterically. How cute we think. These are normal toddler activities aren't they?
  I am asked to come back the next day with my husband.
  Hmm...

- Next day... We are sitting in the Paediatrician's office. Another visiting specialist consultant is sitting in along with the community Paediatric nurse.
  They tell us G has autism.
  I can feel the specialist's eyes burning into me as the other doc is saying about "blah, blah, autistic tendencies... blah, blah..."
  What is going on?? All I can think about is that film Rain Man, and I have a vision of the future of my boy rocking in a corner alone somewhere. I can't hold back the tears anymore and flee the room hotly pursued by the nurse.

Around the time of G's diagnosis we are starting to undergo IVF treatment which will ultimately produce H.
We then returned to West Norfolk where H was born, and we've subsequently stayed in this area to date.
I guess having just had a diagnosis for G I was on the lookout for anything different with H. I asked for an assessment when he was coming up to 2 years old, as I was now sure that H was showing autistic traits of his own, that he wasn't simply copying G. G's behaviours had been similar in some ways; opening and closing doors etc, but different in others. He had never lined up stuff the way H was starting to.

Here's a little taste of G and H from a couple of years back: aged 7 and 4 respectively...

An abbreviated day in the weekday life…
February 2009

2 am   H wakes and climbs into bed with us. Get up and put him back to bed, resetting his music to play on repeat.

3.30am   See above.

5am   See above. G's sleep pattern is also unpredictable, waking between 1 and 5 times a week. He then bounces around downstairs for 2 – 4 hours while I try to kip on the sofa. On the plus side if I couldn't kip I saw quite a few box sets of DVDs during the small hours.

6.30am   G (who is non verbal) wakes up, climbs on our bed then pushes my feet down to the floor to get up. I'm pulled downstairs by the hand to the food cupboard. Manage to get a "stealth hug" in by picking him up and swinging him around. I can count on the fingers of one hand the times he has let me actually kiss his cheek.

7.30am   Play the daily game of struggling to change his nappy as he stops me with his hands, and wriggles his bottom away from me. (Both our boys are still in pads.) He doesn't like being cleaned or touched in this area at all. He refuses to clean teeth, biting the toothbrush. I give him his daily morning medicine by oral syringe, hope he doesn't want to play and spit it out. Around this time H comes downstairs.
Note: H is partly verbal, single words and has echolalia. Echolalia: repeating words, phrases and noises that have been heard.

7.50am   Community transport bus arrives to take G to school, if it's late H gets very upset because G wants shoes on already – we aren't allowed to have shoes or coat on inside the house.

8.20am   Spoon feed H his breakfast. He can bring a loaded spoon to his mouth with encouragement, but if his grip fails and he spills any he gets quite upset, saying "all gone," refusing to eat any more. I keep tissues to hand, if I wipe it clean quick enough I can forestall an "episode" - more on that later folks! He has some sensory issues. Change nappy and get him dressed.

9.30am After taking H to school, morning spent doing the following, delete as applicable:
- Attending meetings / appointments / courses
- Making phone calls to various professionals / volunteers involved with my children
- Attempting to clear the huge pile of filing / paperwork
- Washing / cleaning etc. G doesn't smear so much nowadays, but we still have to wash items soiled with faeces on a regular basis.

    Note: "Smearing" is essentially painting with poo! The reason G doesn't do this so much now is because I limit his access to his own bottom. We have specially made sleepsuits that zip up the back so that he can't strip off his clothes and nappy.

    After that hopefully visit a friend: social contact is a MUST to keep you sane!

1.30pm Try and go for a sleep so I can continue to function.

3pm Pick up H from school. The children's channel CBeebies must always be on the TV while he plays with his cars. After I leave the room he comes out saying "all gone". I spend 10 minutes trying to find out what's wrong before I find a few drops of his drink spilled on his garage.

4pm G arrives home: shoes and coat must come off immediately before H sees, as these are outside clothes and can't be left on indoors. G is given a snack at the table, but as soon as I go to prepare dinner he gets up and bounces round the room. H follows suit getting too close to his brother. He doesn't understand personal space, tries to grab at his neck and gouge his eyes thinking it's a tickle game. I prise them apart, hopefully before G headbutts H causing a full-on brawl. H doesn't like being pulled away so has a wobbly anyway. G covers his ears at the screaming then smacks H to get him to shut up. More screaming and headbutting ensues.

5.30pm Dad arrives home so I can get on with dinner. We all sit and eat, at the same time spoon-feeding H. G finger feeds a range of dry, crunchy foods. This produces an awful lot of extra hoovering! He has no fruit, veg or dairy in his diet and is closely monitored because of this.

6.30pm We forget to lock the bathroom door from the outside. G likes to eat shampoo, toothpaste, Karvol etc. I try to prise the tube of Deep Heat cream from between his teeth without being bitten. I am saving up shampoo bottles with screw tops to use rather than those with the flip-up spouts which make for easy drinking.

7pm Bath time. G has an obsession for 'twiddly' things, chains, ribbons etc. We all play hunt the bath plug as he has run off with the chain. It is finally found in a plant pot in the garden where he had let himself out earlier. Baths are now given separately to the boys as G finds H trying to "help" wash his hair distressing.

7.45pm H screams and thrashes round on the floor because the "Pinky Ponk" is stuck in the tree on one of his DVDs. The "Pinky Ponk" is a kind of airship from the children's programme "In The Night Garden." Things aren't allowed to get stuck or spill, this causes great distress. Also people cheering sound too much like people screaming and it's upsetting to H.

8pm Whilst I'm feeding H his supper, G has sneaked to the kitchen and has to be pulled down from standing on the kitchen surfaces. He is searching with the desperation of a drug addict for any salty crispy snacks. All salty snacks were removed from his diet some time ago. Any cough sweets, his vitamins, any chewy sweets are also fair game. If he gets hold of any sweets he spits out the sucked gooey bits leaving us to scrape the remnants off the carpet.

8.30pm Melatonin is given to G to help him switch off for sleep. Without this he can carry on until 3am.

Melatonin: a hormone that occurs naturally that helps in regulating the sleep cycle. Supplements have been found useful in helping some autistic people switch off for sleep. Unfortunately it doesn't really help with keeping them asleep... well not in my experience!

H is read 2 books at bedtime. Any words or actions inadvertently made during the reading are incorporated into the routine. This must be adhered to strictly or will cause an upset. I made the mistake of kissing him after turning the page once, now we have to do it after every page, the books take twice as long. After this he goes to bed the same way, music has to be playing in his room.

9.30pm G lies across my body to try and sleep. He is often carried up to bed asleep. If put to bed awake I have to dump him and run before he tries to launch himself at me from his raised bed. He has no sense of danger.

Hubby and I grab some time to sit down together before trying to find something different and remotely nutritious for G's lunchbox. He is incredibly picky.

11pm We try and grab some sleep before the youngest comes in around 2am....

Similar but different in the holidays – much more problematic! An abbreviated day in the life: summer holiday 09

2 am H wakes and climbs into bed with us. He used to get between us but has now taken to collapsing across my body pinning me to the bed. As I sleep on my front I can't always wriggle out to put him back, so desperately elbow Steve awake to lift him off me. We put him back to bed, resetting his music to play on repeat.

3.30am See above.

5am   See above. G's sleep pattern is still unpredictable, and may or may not be up for several hours in the night. Steve gets up at 6am for work, but regularly takes his turn in getting up as it's sometimes too exhausting for one person to handle.

6.30am   H gets on to our bed saying "radio." I turn the radio on and H sings over it with nursery rhymes. He likes lots of affection saying "cuddle" and "give me a kiss" repeatedly. When Steve comes into the room he scampers up trying to get to the head of the bed as he doesn't want Steve to take him away from me. Unfortunately he manages to stand on my head in the process. Whatever I say at this point "get off" "careful" etc is repeated gleefully as a game without actually complying. G (non-verbal) wakes up, climbs on our bed and starts to bounce. As H has to mimic G he bounces too, with his own favourite addition: the body slam. I have to wake up and move pretty quickly at this point as he thinks it's great fun to bang his knees and elbows down onto me. H doesn't really know how to play appropriately with G, as G has his own very autistic behaviours such as twiddling his fingers close to his face. This seems to aggravate H who rips G's hands away, trying to gouge at his face with his fingers. G is unpredictable in his response to this, sometimes he'll let it go, others times he'll grab H's hands and dig his fingers into the bones or headbutt him. I try to separate them, while H smacks G around the head. This can degenerate very quickly into a brawl at this point. We all go downstairs very quickly to stop H going into one of his "episodes".

The result of an episode is usually as follows:
Once he's got past the point of no return the tantrum and resulting atmosphere can last for hours. He is incredibly sensitive to tone of voice and a tut under your breath can set him off again, have him thrashing around on the floor on his back whacking his head up and down, yelling swear words. (Ok he might have heard you say something once months ago in a moment of extreme stress!) I can only put him in his room to calm down at this point, and after lots of

8

full-throated screaming, repeated slamming of the door and generally trashing his room the temper seems to go. He then comes out very upset and crying saying "pick up" which I do. He then cries repeatedly into my face "what's the matter", where I have to say "What's the matter? Nothing's the matter, everything's fine" over and over again. H finds certain rituals comforting. The next few hours you are on tenterhooks because although he has calmed down he can very easily flare up again. I constantly have to reassure him, as he keeps getting teary and distressed. I have to say everything in a very happy sing-songy voice like some sort of hammy kids presenter.

7.30am G pulls me by the hand to the food cupboard. I put something out for him on the table that he seems to want. Two minutes later he pulls me to the cupboard again, gets out an identical packet. This goes on for quite a while with me repeatedly putting him back in his chair at the table. Eventually he eats a little. In the meantime I have given H some fruit to keep him occupied. I give both boys a drink but when G has his H whizzes around the table to wrench it out of his hands. Whatever G does H must do, if G has 1 leg tucked under him when sitting so must H. This obsession with G carries over into all parts of his life.

8am Nappy and medicine time. Really could do with some extra octopus-like arms to stop G clamping his hands over his bits and getting mucky.

8.20am Once G has calmed down a bit I can give H his breakfast. He still needs full support when eating with a spoon.

9 am I plan the holidays with a military like precision, trying to get as many activities booked as possible.
These include:
- Days out for G with Mencap which run twice a week for 4 weeks. I try to book our family holiday around these activities. G also goes to his school every day for a week for summer school.

- Gym sessions organised by the local NAS branch at the sports centre twice a week, the boys like to go on the trampoline there.
- Sessions booked at the nursery. I try to give myself 2 days a week where both boys are out 9 – 3pm. The nursery staff are brilliant in accommodating G, as he should be in with the older children. As this club consists of craft / table football / playstation etc it is not appropriate for G, who prefers to have access to the smaller children's outdoor play area / playground. He has his disability buggy in the classroom so he can have a "safe space" of his own. I dread the day when he will be too difficult for the staff to cope with.

11.30am On the days the boys are in nursery I try and go for a sleep so I can continue to function.

3pm Pick up boys from nursery / Mencap / summer school.

4pm Both boys are given a snack at the table, but as soon as I go to prepare dinner G gets up and bounces round the room. H follows suit getting too close to his brother. Damn it!! Cue hands gouging, headbutting and screaming...

5.30pm Dad's home, it's dinner time. I now have to cook sausages and burgers etc for G which is an addition to his diet of dry, crunchy foods. The first time I left some sausages in the oven too long and left them out to cool, it was a real breakthrough diary event when G skipped off with the charcoaled meat. G will now keep trying to get into the oven or grill for the meat, he likes to pick the black bits off the tray. He also likes chocolate bars and cakes, but only the chocolate part. (No, he won't eat a normal milk chocolate bar!) Once he has his food he has a nasty habit of skipping off with it – we often find half eaten sausages and bits of discarded cake and mini chocolate bars around the house, sometimes in our bed. The place is always in a huge mess!

7pm Bath time. We now use a universal camping plug as we got fed up of playing hunt the bath plug when G runs off with the chain.

7.10pm H has emptied an entire bottle of shampoo in the bath so has to have more than the regulation 3 rinses of his hair as it is so soapy. He gets very distressed by this. After Steve has dried him whilst he was kicking and screaming, H stampedes down the stairs, smacks me and falls to the floor thrashing around. Steve takes G out in the pushchair because he finds H's blood-curdling screams distressing.

7.20pm H is still on a fast rotation of saying "pick up... it's all right," standing up then falling to the floor again, shouting "dinner" or "nappy", only to then shout "dinner / nappy finished" immediately after.

8pm The angry screaming has abated slightly to be replaced by bouts of tears. When crying he says "all clean." I must wipe his face with a tissue which he then takes up to flush down the loo. We regularly find whole loo rolls down the toilet. After his face has been cleaned I put on a favourite DVD, all the while talking to him in my best "happy" voice. H is still very sensitive to tone of voice, one of his sensory issues.

8.30pm G has melatonin to help him switch off. H still has 2 books at bedtime. Thankfully I'm now able to read them straight through. In one of his books he once got so fixated with the fact that there was a "buzzy buzzy bee" he could never finish the story properly. After the books he goes to bed the same way, music has to be playing in his room.

9-10 pm G still has to lie across my body in order to get to sleep. It's actually quite nice as it's the one time I get cuddles without having to do it by stealth when tickling him.

11pm I often have a late bath after the boys are asleep, otherwise they insist in climbing in. I let H in with me once but because I wanted to stay in after he came out he threw a wobbly. He has to watch the water go down the plughole.

11.30pm We try and grab some sleep before the youngest one comes in around 2am.…

Due to Hubby's work in the RAF, the nature of the job is that you get posted around the country. The RAF were understanding in that we were able to remain in one place for the boys' sake, as certain things, especially respite, seem to operate on a postcode lottery. Also the boys were very settled and happy in their schools.

Steve remained a functional member of the RAF though, going "out of area" (abroad) for 4 months, then finally having to be posted away from us to the West Midlands. As before though we were able to keep the house at the base in Norfolk, as Steve only had a couple of years left to serve by this time. Yes there were a few sticky points (well ok, incredibly stressful!!) where we were not put on the correct "status." This meant at one time we got a letter to vacate in 28 days. Thankfully the welfare team within the RAF and some good friends on camp saw us through this blip (again, this last sentence covers a world of palpitations!!), and we were put onto the correct housing status. This meant that our position was much more secure.

By the time Steve finished in the RAF he had been doing the weekend commute to us for over 2.5 years.

~~~~~~

Our boys don't have life limiting illnesses. I can't imagine the bittersweet agony of that. But I do savour the precious moments for what they are. Our lads have a lifelong neurological condition with associated learning disability.

When I think about the future, I can picture us; walking with G the man, still taking him to places that we love like the beach and the woods. At the moment the picture I'm slightly wary of is H the man, as he is the one that can't seem to self-regulate his moods, that has the totally unpredictable edge to all his actions. Will he launch the ipod game at my head while I'm driving? As soon as he starts slapping his head the thought skips through my mind and I mentally brace myself!! Will our lads be with us forever? I don't know. Most 'regular' kids leave home eventually (or DO they?!) so some form of independence within sheltered housing or a care home wouldn't necessarily be a bad thing. Just the thought that you may lose one of your children from the family home through being totally unable to cope, or being physically afraid of your son – well that would break my heart.

I love them with every breath in me... or as H would say: "Sooo much!! Gorgeous boy!!!"

I'm not the religious type, so I use the word 'pray' loosely – but I pray that they will be with us as a family as long as we are all around!

I do plan stuff, as we all do for our kids – try to book a holiday, (if you can find somewhere where the fun outweighs the stress!) go out for the day, sort appointments etc. But they are things in the not too distant future. Mostly I take each day or week at a time.

After that first diagnosis all those years ago I was pretty up and down. And yes, it was a kind of grieving for the loss of the dreams of family life that you had. I mean I never had any huge expectations for my boy – or so I thought! I never had visions of him being a brain surgeon or anything.

But I guess I did have a rosy tinted view of what family life might be like, based on my own happy experiences as a child.

I remember walks in the woods with my parents and brothers, wandering freely to pick mushrooms before going home to have them for tea.

Days out on the beach where us kids would wander off to our hearts content; exploring rock pools, splashing in the sea... but we always came back to the blanket so we could share our picnic.

Now it's just different. We go for walks in the woods together, we just generally have to have buggies for when one or both of them refuse to walk anymore! Just... no mushroom picking! G likes to chew at raw mushrooms so probably not a good idea to introduce in a wild setting!

And going to the beach...

I have been able to sit away from people on the beach with H, endlessly throwing pebbles into the sea.

I have paced up and down the shoreline, keeping G firmly on the reins as he gleefully tries to wade out to sea, bending down to lap his tongue at the briny water.

Steve and me generally have a child each here. When I look up from where H is climbing on the groynes near me dropping tiny bits of shell and sand into the water, I see Steve and G running and skipping along the wide Norfolk beach; way, way off in the distance. I feel a deep contentment at these times.

These and other moments make up some magical memories:
Both boys giggling helplessly as the bubbles from the bubble machine shower down over them.
The first time G mimicked my kissing noises, then put his cheek to my mouth for me to kiss. Finally he stunned us by giving us a gentle peck on the lips.
Cuddles from H, hearing his little voice for the first time, then the first times he actually started to comment on things, not just to parrot them.
H crooking his little index finger in a hook from his fist, to point at things.
Watching G intensely lose himself in a patch of long grass, flicking his fingers in front of his scrunched up eyes at full speed. Then later, giving me full on arms round the neck hugs.

This started out as a kind of reference for myself, of behaviours, of things said or done in response to something that showed a different understanding from mine.
Being alone with my boys for a good portion of the time this was written, it also morphed into a kind of therapy for me. I hope you don't feel I'm laughing at my boys here; rather, I'm trying to find humour in a sometimes untenable situation. As the saying goes, if you don't laugh, you'll cry!
There have been many times when I've laughed with them believe me, and sometimes they laugh at me too.
I just ask that you please try not to judge me too harshly as a mother: I am doing the best I can on very little sleep, and I know I've failed spectacularly at times. I am, however, only human: the same as our 2 lovely lads. We are all just trying to find a way to be a family in harmony.

At the beginning of writing:
G: 10 years, 10 months
H: 6 years 11 months
Me: 44 years, 1 month

Chapter 1:

It's good to talk... or to write...

A friend very kindly used to chat to me online. When I was struggling for understanding, or just frustrated, she was a sounding board for me. I guess I can thank her for getting me used to writing things down, firstly to relate as an example, then for myself as a reference.
These simple diary entries slowly morphed into a kind of therapy for me. After all, it did help to see the funny side, sometimes!

June 2011
Unprovoked apology

Although the boys are both on the autistic spectrum, they are very, very different. For a while now H has had a tendency to attack G when G does something, or acts some way that doesn't make sense to H. We have been working on this, constantly trying to reinforce the good behaviour: "Good boys for playing nicely together!!"

After being told off yet again for attacking G, H goes into meltdown. Every time they go outside to bounce I say "play nicely together." H repeats this before going out and slamming the door.
This time after H has got upset and wants a cuddle I say "You need

to play nicely together."
H strokes G's hair and says "Sorry G."

Ok I know this doesn't seem a big deal, but it was sufficiently amazing that I had to write it down. Normal behaviour for H was clawing and gouging at G's face, whacking and kicking him. It was quite nice that he seemed to give some consideration for G.

10th July 2011
"You want the drink."

There are 2 bottles of drink on the table by G's seat, 1 red, 1 orange.
H is holding the red bottle, getting increasingly agitated until I get up and go towards him.
H: "You want the drink."
Me: "You've got the drink."
H: "You want the drink!"
Me: "You want the orange drink?" (offering orange drink.)
H: "Table."
H gives me the red drink, I put it on H's side of the table. (About 3 feet away.)
H then picks up the red drink again.
I guess he wanted me to give him the bottle.

I feel here that H was beginning to see me as an extention of himself, or as a tool for his use.

10th July 2011
Bath time.

G is chilling out playing in the bath, after I've just changed a rather full dirty nappy. H is kicking off as he needs a new nappy so I go downstairs to see to him.
Five minutes later I go back up to find a gleeful G in the bath with the cold tap running on full, turds floating everywhere.
The water is the colour of chocolate with quite a high cocoa content. Doesn't smell quite as nice though.

Luckily I have an old slotted spoon for straining veg that belonged to Mum ready for this situation, and manage to scoop out approximately 3 more sausages worth of poo.

At least I can put the paediatrician's mind at rest as far as G's bowel movements go.

21st July 2011
Ferry trip - total ecstasy!

We are so lucky in that we have relatives who take pity on us (!!) and invite us to stay so they can share caring for the boys, and of course they love to see them too.

We are on the high speed ferry to Jersey and G has dragged me outside onto the deck, I have him on his heavy duty reins.

The ferry is really whizzing along now, with a huge wake of spray shooting up.

We stagger and lurch from one side of the deck to the other, cackling madly. This is so infectious, G is now pressing his face against the railings, licking the salt off, shaking his head wildly from side to side laughing into the spray and the wind! We are getting soaked but I just don't care!! I wish I could bottle this moment!

26th August 2011
Stress-free shopping

The time was when H would happily go into the "big shop" (supermarket) with me and sit in a trolley nicely as long as he had a load of grapes to munch on.

Not anymore.

In the supermarket I start looking for the bits I need. Suddenly H yells "Eggs, Mummy get eggs!"

H likes words and letters. I quickly realise that he is checking out the overhead aisle signs, the first one having "Eggs" on it, a word he knows.

I am trying to get the fruit and veg I wanted but within seconds H is freaking out about the eggs, wanting a cuddle, gripping me around the neck so I can't straighten up again.

I say "Mummy get eggs" and proceed to the egg bit, still hunched over with little hands around my neck. I show him the box.
H: "Eggs open" - I hold the box away from him and open the box to show him the eggs.
I then put the eggs back.
He is happy again.

I try to carry on shopping... until the next random word catches his eye.
"Mummy get baby." (Not on your life, 2 kids are enough!!)
I grab some baby wipes or anything with the word "baby" on. All ok again.
I am forgetting what I wanted now, with demands for various objects coming thick and fast. I really must make a list next time...
Next comes "Mummy get Graydr..." something something...?
At this point I am at a loss. We are in the confectionery aisle.
I say "Show Mummy the Graydr.." whatever.
He pulls me toward some chocolate, and I realise it's the stylized word "Cadbury" he is trying to read.
I segment the syllables reading the word, which makes him happy again.
Feeling slightly frazzled now and I'm not sure if I've got all I wanted, but what the hell, we've all had enough!

H's behaviour really did change from one shopping trip to the next. It's impossible to predict when the next obsession or anxiety will appear and what form it will take!
Since this incident we introduced an iPod touch, known to H as the "Phone game." He plays games like Angry Birds that seem to focus his attention a little, rather than fixating on every sign, hoarding, and product he can see with wording on.

27th August 2011
DON'T change your mind!

H is getting increasingly demanding in wanting to know exactly where we are going and what we are doing in advance, every day. If we say we are doing something then we MUST follow through as at this point he is totally unable to cope with change.

Every morning first thing, H asks "We're going...?"
Today Steve is home so he tells H we're going to town.
Unfortunately we didn't need to go after all and decided to try and
get around it by saying "Driving through the town, then garden
centre."
H then asked for "snack" (Doritos), but we didn't have any so I
ignored this and gave him something else. We are still in the car, H is
watching "Something Special" (a programme that introduces
makaton sign language for children) on his DVD and constantly
wants me to repeat parts of the dialogue back to him, ("Granddad
Tumble!") saying "That's right" at the end.
I am trying to ignore this as the Occupational Therapist says it's
controlling behaviour. However H is having none of it and is craning
his face round to look into mine, whilst getting increasingly stressed
and repeating the words louder and louder.
Eventually I crack and yell back "GRANDDAD TUMBLE...
THAT'S RIGHT!!"
This doesn't really improve the atmosphere.

We go into the garden centre cafe to have lunch but as soon as we
are there H starts full-on screaming. Steve takes him out in the buggy
while I eat with G, then returns. H is still crying, asks to get out of
the buggy, then does his banging down onto his knees routine.
He thrashes around on the floor in the cafe for a few minutes then
asks for a "cuddle" (death grip around the neck) then "wipe your
face." (I give him a tissue.)
Things are slightly calmer when H starts obsessing about "red"
pepper. The pepper we have is green and yellow, and he has never
worried about the different colours before.
H is in a state of high stress all the way home until he can have some
red pepper.

2nd September 2011
"We're going on a journey."

I am really blessed in that I have a personal assistant for a set number of hours a month to use in any way that helps us. I'm going to name her... 'Marianne.'
She is known to the boys as Marianne, as that's the way she first introduced herself to us, so for the boys that's her name. She is known to me by the name her friends and family use; Annie.
This particular day Hubby isn't around so Annie has come along to help so we can actually go out.

This morning I didn't know how busy Pizza Hut would be so didn't want to say ahead of time in case we couldn't get in... instead I told H we were going "on a journey."
I thought he had accepted this as an activity the way he used to accept "going for a drive" as an answer in itself... but no. Big mistake.
We get to Pizza Hut.
H: "Journey, get journey!"
Managed to distract him for a bit with lunch, then...
"Journey!" (Getting quite upset here.)
Me: "We're going to the Boots shop" (as in the chemist.)
H then started yelling "Mummy get boots!" Was placated with a Boots card that he could read the word on.
After shopping...
"Journey!!" (More screaming, tears and general confusion.)
We get back in the car and I tell him: "We're on a journey, then going home. Journey first, then home."
So we get home... he's really upset now: "JOURNEY!!! You want cuddle..." etc, etc.
I draw a picture of a car going along the road and write the word "journey" above it, showing H. This is obviously not helping matters.
I also try writing a simple visual timetable showing "Dinner, then journey, then home."
H is getting increasingly stressed and trying to control the situation. (Probably doing quite a good job of it too.)
Eventually we all get in the car to take Annie home. All the way I am saying "Journey, then Marianne's house... journey, then Marianne's house..."
When we get there, I say "Marianne's house." But you guessed it...

"JOURNEY!!"
Finally we get one of Annie's dogs to come near H, and we call it "Journey"... "This is Journey, Hello Journey..." etc.
H says hello to "Journey," then goodbye, then we go home again.
Well, it worked.

4th September 2011
"Dollar – Snack"

For a couple of months now H has had a thing for a particular song: "I need a dollar" by Aloe Black. He has also asked for it out of the blue in times of stress.
Lately I have noticed that he appears to have made a link in his mind between the song ("Dollar") and "snack" (Doritos).
Today in the soft play area the song came on the radio. I looked out for H, and sure enough he was hurriedly making his way back towards us.
"Dollar snack, Mummy get dollar snack!" Managed to fob him off with a couple of crisps we had, he repeated about the "snack" a couple of times but then thankfully let it drop.
This could be due to a couple of things: maybe he was eating snack the first time he heard the song and took a shine to it, or (I think this may be more likely) he has seen the stylized writing of the word "Doritos" on the "snack" packet and thinks it looks like the way the word "dollar" is spelt, and has made a connection.
They said on the NAS (National Autistic Society) Early Bird course that you need to "be a detective" to find out what our children are thinking... H definitely keeps throwing up some weird things for us to figure out...

10th September 2011
A trip to town

Wheeling the buggies into Primark, H asks "We're going...?"
Me: "We're going in the clothes shop."
H: "Clothes... H get clothes on!"
Me: "No clothes on... we're looking at clothes!"

H: "Clothes on... seatbelt off" (quite agitated now and wanting to come out of the buggy).

I let him out of the buggy, he grabs the first thing to hand – a woman's yellow vest top. He insists in putting it on over his own clothes, he's struggling a bit so I help him. Then I say "Take clothes off again" which we do.

(In the meantime G has acquired some ear muffs which he refuses to take off until we get back to the car later.)

H then says several times increasingly urgently: "Mummy get up." I think he means to pick up things off the floor. (This is a shop where people tend to chuck stuff around after all!) He is getting quite stressed now so we quickly distract him with the "phone game" (Angry Birds).

The rest of the trip around the shop passes without a hitch, when we come out I say "Phone game finished, we're walking around the town." H complies with this.

Next we go into a sweet shop to see if I can get a treat for G, as he is the one that loves sweets. However as soon as we are in H starts asking for sweets, trying to pull my hand towards the glass counter where the sweets are. He is getting agitated very quickly, I buy a single sweet for 6p for him so I can continue to look at leisure. This seems to do the trick.

We then look in a cook shop. When we tell him this H says "Mummy get cook." I am fast realising that H's logic tells him he needs whatever item is mentioned. I pick up a spoon and tell H "Mummy got the cooking tool."

This seems to placate him.

In the street H says "3 store, that's right." I realise he has read the shop name and say well done, before realising to my horror there are huge posters of 'Angry Birds' in the window (a game H really likes). A second later... "Angry birds, Mummy get angry birds!"

Me: "We've had angry birds today, we're walking around the town!"

(If you say things like this in a sing-song jokey voice you may just get away with it!)

On the way back to the car we pass the ice-cream van. He's already had one earlier; this doesn't stop him asking for another one! We deal with this in the same way – sing-song voice time.

He smiles.

Normal life!

I had made friends after attending the National Autistic Society's Early Bird course, one of whom also happened to be at the same RAF base as us. She helped me out when Steve was away for 4 months, asking me round for tea etc just so I could get out of the house with the boys. I had an other-worldly kind of life then, as G was up springing around for around 4 hours most nights while I watched box sets of Star Trek Voyager, Next Generation and the like. I'd actually been queuing up outside nursery one day, closed my eyes for a second, then found myself jerking awake moments later. (Thankfully without any drool escaping from my lolling mouth.)

Slowly I got to know some other "autism Mums" via a support group who have since become very good friends. I'd also dragged myself out to Mums and Tots in the early days and was lucky enough to make a friend who subsequently dragged me down to the Thrift shop (a kind of charity shop) to volunteer. It was the Thrift that was probably my first foray into a "regular" community outside our autism related, sleep deprived little world. Just chatting to "regular" people about their "regular" kids was a little break from what was happening at home. These people that became my friends really took my boys to their hearts, they didn't necessarily know much about autism but just accepted them for who they are, and understood that it was a struggle sometimes. The Thrift became part of our weekly routine on the evening it was open; I would take the boys down there, help out a little and have some adult interaction while the other volunteers would be bouncing and jumping with my lads; watching all the exits, naturally!

15th September 2011
Communication

We are in the Thrift Shop again to stop G going stir crazy, and to let H play with the toys!

H: " H, ball, Thrift Shop.... that's right."

He insists I say "that's right."
I then see him go into a ball pool. I'm unsure whether he was asking permission, or just telling me what he was going to do.

16th September 2011
More communication: Lid off

We are in the car going to school.
H starts getting agitated, saying "Lid off, Mummy get lid off." His school bottle that he has on the way home has a lid.)
I think he is asking for a drink, but as I go to get his bottle from his bag he pulls my hand towards the integral cup holder in his car seat.
I help push the cup holder away into the seat and all is fine again.

20th September update:
H has done the "lid off" routine a couple of times now. Today in the car on the way home he said "Lid on." (wanting the cup holder out. I very clearly said "Cup holder" then "cup holder out" demonstrating this. H repeated "lid on... that's right" a few times, increasingly agitated.
Unfortunately H has made the rather skewed connection between wanting a drink and putting the bottle in the cup holder, and this now appears to be fixed in his mind.

16th September 2011
Throwing things

H has had PE in the afternoon where he has been practising throwing and catching. We are walking out from the school grounds when H accidentally kicks a large stone lying on the path. He then immediately picks up the stone.
Cue one of those kind of slow motion moments - just as I am yelling "H, NO!!" he launches the stone high in the air, arcing down and landing on the shoulder of a girl walking in front of us.
Me: "We don't throw stones! We don't throw stones!!! That hurt Cathy!" (I have hastily asked the name of the girl so that H can apologise to her.)

H looks a little bemused by this.

The next couple of minutes I'm telling H to say sorry to Cathy. H seems rather confused and mouths the words under his breath. There is a bit of a stony silence during this from the girls grandfather, now comforting the sobbing girl, while the mother says don't worry it's ok.

I apologise profusely, if my face gets any redder it's going to spontaneously combust.

We move away after a few minutes and walk back to the car. Halfway there H says "Cleaning the Cathy" and tries to pull back the way we have come.

I say "Cathy was crying, she was hurt but she's fine now."

H needs to "clean" things when they get dirty; this includes tears on children's faces. As he doesn't have much idea of what a gentle touch is I tend not to let him too near other children!

16th September 2011
Escape Artist

Some autistic children seem to have the trait of being "runners." You need eyes in the back of your head and an ability to sprint and rugby tackle dive if necessary as a lack of danger awareness can also be a factor. The first time this was driven home to me was when G was waiting at the car door to get in when we were on holiday. I was just opening the door to get H in. G was crouched down fiddling with some grass when he suddenly upped and bolted for the cliff edge approximately 30 metres away.

I am far from small but my God I shifted that day!

Once you've got a "runner" you really need to re-think your surroundings. We keep all doors locked, the keys for those doors further locked into another key cabinet or cupboard with a high bolt. Non-climbable fences, nothing butted up against them to use as handy stepping stones.

Now, that is. You do learn not to take their safety for granted, but sometimes even the most wary of us are lulled into a false sense of security... then the little beggars will grab their chance!

Oh and by the way, my lad has autism, which by no means equates to a lack of crafty intelligence. He is more than capable of moving objects to enable him to climb to those pesky hard to reach spots where I have hidden toiletries, cough sweets, door keys...

G is now routinely climbing the wire at the corner of the garden to go into next door's. Thankfully they are ok with this, constantly bringing him back. Today he hopped the fence again while I was cooking; my neighbour said he was fine just come and get him when I've finished cooking. I've nearly finished cooking when I get a phone call to say he is now in next-door-but-one's garden on their trampoline. He has been in their sprinkler, tried to strip but then (thankfully) changed his mind, run upstairs and nicked a pack of chewing gum.

We have now rigged up a couple of fence posts with small gauge chicken wire over them.

Maybe it will work. Watch this space.

17th September 2011
Vocabulary

I have just got out of the shower and have wet hair.
H: "Bath head!"

In the car we pass under a net of wires stretched under the pylons.
H: "Big wire chair... that's right."

A bucket of coal: "Grandpa's black eggs!" - Grandpa has a coal fire. And I guess the coke looks like eggs, a little.

20th September 2011
Memory

H is getting a little too "hands on" with G, trying to hit him in the face. I pull him away saying "You don't hit G, sit down." I make him sit on the sofa.

5 minutes later he starts whimpering, wanting "cuddle" and "pick

up."

Then: "You want X, you want X on the fridge."

Let me explain: ages ago H had some singing magnet letters for the fridge, but one day when putting the letters in order we discovered X was missing. A big meltdown ensued at the time. I guess having an upset today reminded him of an upset another time, albeit over a year ago!

I divert H to a laptop toy that has letters and press the X button. Crisis averted.

27th September 2011
A day in the life...

H has been coming into our bed since he was 3 years old. He started this when we were away one Christmas staying at my in-laws. We had stayed there many times before so I'm not sure what triggered this; I tried returning him back to his own bed each time for about 18 months before giving up! I was getting so tired towards the end of the night I wasn't waking up any more.

I invested in a heavy draught excluder with a cat's head (named "Bed-cat") to keep him on his side of the bed, which helped a little.

1am
H comes in to my bed, saying "radio on". I put the radio on the lowest possible volume setting and put my earplugs back in.

2am
G comes squeaking into my bedroom. It's earlier than usual for him. All the lights are on downstairs where he's been looking for food. I make another mental note to myself to phone the assistive living people about the broken door exit sensors in his bedroom.

5am
Have been dozing on and off and wake to find G laid across my legs. I leave my bed to him and H and go to kip in G's room.

6.30am
H is awake.
H: "Mummy get downstairs."

I buy myself approximately 20 minutes by asking for a cuddle etc and saying "Mummy's having a rest!"

3.20pm

I have to go to the loo after picking H up at school because I've been swilling tea and Pepsi all day to keep awake. We go in and I belatedly realise the hand dryer is out of order.

H: "Dryer not working... dryer high up (the switch)... dryer is fine..." etc. We go out and see the cleaners in the corridor. Yesterday I mentioned to a cleaner about the hand dryer.

H: (pulling me to a halt and making me face the cleaners) "Hiya... dryer not working... dryer is fine..." I explain to the ladies about the dryer. We head out back to the car. There is a group of 3 mums on the pavement. H pulls me to a stop and pushes my face towards them and gives his "dryer" spiel again. Obviously hasn't got it out of his system. I'm hoping we don't have to stop and tell any more random groups of people.

4pm

We are all back home, H wants the "phone game". While I get it I forget the key is still in the back door – G is out and over next doors fence by the time I get out after him. I go to get some stuff to entice him with and stand at the end of our garden shouting "G... Doritos... sweets!"

This fails miserably. H runs out in a stress to tell me the phone's ringing. When I turn back to G he has disappeared into the garden 2 doors down with the trampoline (yes I know, it's not like we don't have a bigger one). I can see his head bouncing up and down over the fence.

I make another apologetic trip to the neighbours and have to physically drag him out again.

5.30pm

I am checking some emails sitting at the computer desk. G sits down on the floor. He likes to pull my feet into his tummy, constantly pushing them off his lap, then pulling them back into his tummy again. However, lately he has been wanting to pull my feet hard into his groin. Thankfully he is still padded so I am unable to tell what is going on down there. I hastily move my feet away!

6pm

H and G come inside, H pushing G along and saying "G need new nappy" over and over.

I check G and say "G doesn't need new nappy, G is fine."

H says "G new nappy" again, then "G socks off." He gets quite upset when I don't change G. Meanwhile G is grabbing my hand and arm to gouge me with his fingernails, he often draws blood. Another note to self: trim G's nails. He is quite susceptible to my tone of voice when I am being assertive with H.

I soon realise that H is actually the one that needs the nappy and has wet socks so I sort him out. He says "You want sleep" and "Mummy having a rest". He says this sometimes after getting emotional. He calms down a little but is still very agitated until I change G's nappy.

6.30pm

One of my helpers comes to take the boys to her house for a couple of hours. I cook something for myself that isn't microwaveable or toast, and catch up on a bit of telly. Oh, and have a cup of tea without H gleefully dropping food debris into it. Bliss!

8.30pm

The boys are back and dressed ready for bed. The plan is that H is ready to have his book and then go to bed as soon as they get back. Unfortunately they accidentally bumped heads when they were playing together at my helper's house, and though they had lots of cuddles and distraction, and they thought it was all sorted - H doesn't forget. It's like he NEEDS to have a meltdown.

Before I realise what he is going to do he goes up behind G and headbutts the back of his head. Luckily my helpers are still with me so they comfort G while I sort H out for bed.

H: "Hurt G... Mummy cuddle G" (This is to make it better. Very thoughtful except it would have been better not to nut G in the first place.) He then throws himself on the floor and thrashes around a bit, asking for "cuddle".

I think I've calmed him down when he asks for a certain "disk". I turn the DVD player on for about 10 seconds, enough to be able to then say "Disk finished, H do book."

Finally we can move on to the next step in the bedtime routine and all is fine.

8.50pm
On finishing the book I say "Book finished." This used to suffice, until last night.
H: "Book finished, then...?"
Me: "Then bed."
H: "then...?"
Me: "Then sleep."
H: "Then...?"
Me: "Then wake up, then breakfast, then school."
H: "School bag! Bye Mummy!"
He is obviously looking forward to going to school.

9.30pm
G had his melatonin about half an hour ago and is now asleep. Unfortunately I was speaking on the phone to my Father-in-law, when the window of opportunity for getting G up to bed awake passed. I haul him up the stairs and flop him into bed. Getting a bit more of a struggle to do this as he's surprisingly heavy for a very small 10 year old. Thankfully these days he "asks" to go to bed about 50% of the time so I don't have to lug his dead weight upstairs.
Really could do with him having a lower bed... oh and maybe a stairlift...

Relating to the hand dryer associated ritual

27th September 2011
Went in the disabled toilet at school with H at the end of the day. All was fine until I went to dry my hands and the hand dryer didn't work.
H: "Dryer on!"
I put my hand up to the switch on the wall to make sure it's actually turned on. It was.
Me: "Dryer's broken, dryer not working."
He got a little agitated but was generally ok.
We came out of the loo to meet one of the cleaners about to go in. I said about the dryer not working as she looked like she was going to use the loo, she said she wasn't, just cleaning etc. We chatted for a moment then went.

28th September 2011

Went into the loo again, said again about the dryer not working etc. We are leaving when we see a different bunch of cleaners by their store cupboard. H drags me to a halt and mimics my words to the cleaner from yesterday... we also had to say "dryer not working... dryer is fine... dryer high up..." etc as that was similar to what I had said to him in the loo!

On the way out of school a bunch of mums are standing chatting on the pavement. He stops me again and is very insistent in pushing my face round with his hands as if to talk to them and says the dryer stuff again. (Thankfully they don't notice... it's bad enough all the cleaners think we're head cases!)

19th October 2011 update

I am now having to go in the loo at school whether I want to or not!! H appears to need to do the whole "dryer broken" thing.

I am going to ask if I can pick up H where I drop him in the morning to try and cut out that ritual, as the loo is not so close by as at the other exit.

Unfortunately due to sleep deprivation I spend a lot of my daylight waking hours swigging tea and Pepsi Max to keep myself going, which is how I've come to need the loo in the first place.

Note to self: invest in large cork.

1st October 2011
Empathy

We are in the play area by the woods. There is a German family there, the little girl is crying noisily. H watches her for a few minutes. Suddenly, H pulls me towards her: "Girl hurt, cuddle girl, Mummy cuddle girl."

Me: "Girl is fine."

H: "Girl hurt." He is still pulling towards the girl, who is shrinking away from him, crying harder. I tell the Dad he is just worried about the little girl, he is very patient and seems to understand. I'm keeping H away from the girl as I'm not sure at this point if he will hit her or "stroke" her. He falls down to the ground and lies on his back, whining and repeating "Cuddle girl!"

Me: "Girl's Daddy cuddling girl."

H gets up and pulls me towards the family again.

H: "Daddy cuddle girl."

He reaches out and strokes the Dad's arm, "Aaah... soft! Daddy cuddle girl."

Me: "The Daddy is cuddling girl, girl is fine."

I then distract him by telling him to play on the slide.

Guten Tag, welcome to Norfolk!

4th October 2011
Early Morning

It's a very warm night; I become aware of G coming in my room, it's 4am. He is a little squeaky so I take him back to his room. I go into H's bed as he was already in mine, but H joins me in his again. Gets too crowded and hot so I go back to my bed, H follows. He sits up in my bed and shows way too many signs of waking up properly.

The next couple of hours pass with H wriggling about, saying "Mummy sleep, H sleep, that's right" and generally fidgeting about and making a noise.

6am ish: G has been back on the bed with H and me for around half an hour, being a bit giggly. H keeps getting right next to him and trying to play. Then he realises that G is chewing a bottle top or something.

"G, spit it out, spit it out G!"

Me: "G is fine..." etc.

H started getting a bit too in G's face, grabbing his hands, telling me to cuddle G etc. Then he started to kick G with his feet and I smacked his leg (no, I'm not proud of it!) then put him in his room.

H had the predictable meltdown, though not straight away. Gradually slid off the bed, then went through a round of jumping and banging down on his knees and head etc, with a large amount of head slapping (his own).

"Clean the knee... hurt your head... cuddle... you want Granddad's house..." etc.

Eventually calmed him down, then gave him the phone game and sat him on the sofa.

8th October 2011
"Cuddle the stone."

Went to our empty house today: the house we are trying to sell. H decides to pick up a stone and throw it near the neighbour's car.
Me: Taking him inside, "We don't throw stones... let's watch the castle, shapes, art disk (a favourite DVD).
H: Pulling me back out of the door, "Stone, Mummy cuddle the stone..."
Me: (Can't believe I'm doing this...) Picking up a stone, "There, Mummy cuddled the stone."
H: "Stone is fine... that's right."
Since this incident, among other things I have had to "cuddle" the pushchair, my bed (after G spilled a tube of gel over it) and a pair of H's socks after they got wet.

8th October 2011
Don't use adjectives

Around this time we were selling the house we owned, and needed to go periodically to mow the lawn, weed the patio, pick up the post etc. This house was empty. Usually hubby would go on his own but this time there was stuff to do in Norwich afterwards so we all decided to go.

So I thought I was doing the right thing writing down the timetable of events for today:
"Drive, then empty house, then Norwich town, then home."
I get a sense of things to come when we are at the "empty house."
H: "Empty... Empty's knocking at the door." (Oh dear.)
We go through the timetable, get home, then:
"Empty's coming to play!"

Time for a distraction: phone game!

12th October 2011
The wet clothes and new nappy connection

G has spilt some juice on the carpet. I try to rub the drips away with my feet before H sees and has a flap about it. He notices this.
H: "Socks off, Mummy socks off."
I take them off.
H: "New nappy, Mummy have new nappy!"
Me: "Mummy doesn't have a nappy!"
A bit of distraction follows as I tickle him with my feet.

22nd October 2011
Misplaced Empathy?

H is watching an animated programme about cartoon birds. They have a cake making machine that gets broken.
H, upset, in tears: "Cake broken!"
Cue cuddles, reassurance: "Look, they are fixing the cake machine, cake machine is fine."

22nd October 2011
Changing expectations

Have tried to remember most of the details of H's language and behaviour etc, but there was an awful lot happening almost simultaneously.

We are at the seaside, we take the boys into the soft play centre. Sadly, they seem to be closing an hour early, and therefore we have missed the 'last admissions' time.
H is champing at the bit to get out of the pushchair and into the play zone.
Me: "Soft play is closed, we're going to the beach."
Lots of screaming and thrashing around from H ensues. We manage to get out of the place, H screaming and bucking all the way.
"Soft play! Seatbelt off! Pick up! Cuddle!"
After lots of death grip cuddles around the neck of both Steve and I, we push on. H seems calm enough to be let out of the pushchair. A

minute later we get to the ramp to the beach.

H: "Pushchair down." We go down the slope. On arriving at the shore H picks up some sand. I think he is going to throw it in the water but he shoves it down his nappy.

H, very agitated now: "New nappy, trousers off, clean, beach shower..." He then bangs down on his knees on the sand, causing even more upset as he then needs the trousers cleaned.

We change his nappy with some difficulty as he wants to lie down on the sand and I won't let him, as I know this will make things far worse. (Don't really want to give him a beach shower in late October.)

H refuses to put his trousers back on: "You want red trousers, red trousers on!!" It dawns on me that he means his pyjamas. He also has a go at pulling my hair to try and "hurt Mummy."

Me: "Pushchair, then home, then red trousers." This doesn't go down well.

I eventually manage to manhandle him back into the buggy, despite H's protests: "Work buggy!" (I'm not sure what this means, maybe fix or clean??) By the way that sentence was quite easy to write... the reality of getting him into the buggy was decidedly NOT easy.

We get off the beach, H screaming all the way. He then wants seatbelt off again, and stupidly we let him as he then runs back towards the soft play, yelling at the top of his lungs. Hubby gets him. This leads to more struggling, death grip cuddles around the neck and requesting "pick ups." About half an hour has passed at this point.

Much earlier (whilst still happy) H had noted "Seaside: chips!"

Now we arrive at the chip shop, we get a portion to share and go to a table. (That sentence sounded quite straightforward. It actually involved more screaming and struggling, etc.) H, still with no trousers on) bangs first one knee then the other on the ground. "Hurt H!"

Then hits Steve's stomach: "Hurt Daddy!" Then rubs Steve's head, "Poor Daddy!"

Meanwhile he has been asking for tissue to wipe his face; unfortunately this hasn't been enough to resolve the matter as he can't seem to move on. We offer him chips: "No chips!" G however is nibbling on chips quite nicely which is kind of a diary event for him.

We somehow get H's trousers back on.
He is now glued to my lap, whilst struggling constantly, lolling around with his head towards the ground, asking again for "red trousers."
"Sleep!" Then whipping my glasses off, "Mummy sleep!"
We cuddle for a minute.
"Sun off, you want sleep."

I write on a piece of paper a simple timetable of events to try and alleviate things: car, then home, then red trousers etc. We manage to get back to the car with the minimum amount of screaming. We make a stop at the playground on the way home, G gets out to play. After about 10 minutes despite saying he wanted sleep H gets out for a bit. An hour has now passed and things have finally got calmer. I realise that I was going to go to the toilet in the soft play centre but I still haven't gone. Never mind, will wait until we get home!

Things seem ok again at home, H is playing on the phone game.
H: "Jab out, Mummy get jab out."
Me: "Jab out?? Show Mummy the jab out." (I try this when I have no idea what he is talking about.)
H, repeatedly: "Jab out, Mummy jab out!" Then, "Marianne white phone game."
Me: "No Marianne today, H's phone game."
H: "Jab out, phone game!!"

Let's just say it degenerates from there, until H throws the phone game on the floor. I drag him upstairs to his room. Lots of screaming, banging down on knees, slapping his head... etc. REALLY distressed.
(Suddenly realize I still haven't been to the loo so grab the opportunity!) After a couple of minutes I let him out of his room, we go downstairs. H wants me to "cuddle the downstairs/floor" – I guess because he 'hurt' the floor when he threw the phone game. H asks for a disk amid much crying and distress. He watches the disk for a minute while I put him in PJs.

He's expecting porridge, so I prepare it. He asks for grapes and porridge, so he has a few grapes but then says porridge finished.

I read him his book (while he is still crying on and off) then clean his teeth. He then takes himself downstairs again, asking for disk. I take him upstairs amid more struggling and crying to put him to bed. He usually has music playing, but H now says "Music sleep, Mummy get disk." He turns the CD player upside-down. Ok that's fairly clear.

We get the DVD player and put the disk on to play in his room and say goodnight.

It's been 4 hours since the soft play thing happened.

24th October 2011
Sunday night/Monday morning waking pattern

Hubby has been doing the weekly commute to work for around 18 months now, "coming to play" on Friday evening, going back to work on Sunday night. Not sure if the Sunday night routine is just about Daddy or if it's a general combo of not having had the structure of school all weekend.

G was up at 2am again, this is the third week running I think.
Week 1: awake at 2am... stayed up until he slept at school.
Week 2: awake at 2-3am... back to sleep approx 6.30am.
Week 3: Today – awake at 2am... back to sleep around 5.30am
Today, no school as we are on half term. Will see what happens next week.

24th October 2011
Exaggerated tics

H has been tapping/slapping his head on and off for some time now. (since early summer?) The last 3 – 4 weeks I have noticed a new tic, he does little short sharp hums under his breath, often whilst bringing his closed hands up to his cheeks.

26th October 2011
Half term holiday: "We're going home!"

We have come to stay with Granddad as we often do in the school holidays. We have been there one night. This is the first time he has persistently wanted to go home, and then back to school.

H: "We're going home!"

Me: "We're at Granddad's house!"

I then get a piece of paper and pen and write out "Granddad's house... sleep" in a box then repeat this across the page, writing the names of the days across the top. I then read this to H, following my finger so he can see. Then I count how many times the word "sleep" has been written.

Over the next few days H asks for "Home... then wake up to the school!" several times a day. I am able to say "3 sleeps (e.g.) at Granddad's, then home."

He does seem to be placated by this, at least until the next time he asks!

Things at home were a little more complicated than usual at this point – we were house hunting!! Oh joy! The RAF house we were in, well we were entitled to stay there until the end of March 2012. So we really needed to find a house. (As hubby was due out of the RAF the following January it would also be good to be settled before then. Didn't fancy job and house-hunting at the same time.)

Trouble is, the money we had available and the things on our wish list weren't very compatible! We were looking for a 'forever' house, in that it was going to be painful enough to move once so we didn't want to do it again when we outgrew the place.

Therefore a nice big place was in order, with an extra room available so I could do a kind of sensory/chill out room. Let's face it the boys are always going to be with us, and years down the line we are going to have 2 strong, strapping young men with a very different set of needs.

Oh and a big garden would be nice, I do like to grow a bit of veg.

Oh and I'd quite like a couple of chickens again one day…

A girl can dream can't she?!

Chapter 2:

"There may be trouble ahead..."

31st October 2011
Meltdown in the car

It's the Monday after half term, I've picked H up from school and we are on our way home.

H: "Home then phone game!" I agree.
Then: "Home then...?
Me: "Home then phone game, then tea time, then Marianne's coming to play."
H, laughing a little: "Marianne is...? Marianne's at the door!"
Me, laughing: "Marianne's not at the door yet!"
He repeats "Marianne's at the door!" a few times, getting increasingly agitated.

Cue lots of asking for cuddles, tears, etc, building up to full on screaming. We are driving through the village when H lets himself out of the seatbelt and starts pulling at me, I pull in to a driveway where he proceeds to pull at the car seat, open the door, throw out the drink lid which he has managed to unscrew. By this time he is not placated by the cuddle which I give him, he keeps pulling me back down with a death-grip around my neck.

I somehow get the seatbelt back on and pull away despite him having fistfuls of my hair and manage to shut his door. He then repeatedly opens the door. I'm afraid by this point I am yelling back at him to sit down etc.

I finally get back in and continue driving... next thing I know H is pulling at my hands and arms, whips my glasses off and throws them. I pull up sharpish and stick the hazard lights on. (Yes, I am as blind as a bat.) I'm afraid this time I am really screaming at him, "Danger!" and "Sit down!" etc, and yes, it is peppered with the f word as I am really quite stressed by this time (notice the understatement). I'm not proud of myself but there you are.

I grope around for my glasses, only to find one of the lenses has fallen out. I realise I have blood on my hands from my face – H is now yelling about that as well as everything else. The side of my nose is bleeding due to having my glasses ripped off of it.

Luckily my prescription sunglasses are in the car so I don't have to drive the rest of the way home with one eye squeezed shut to avoid the double vision / inebriated feeling. Yay – bonus!! Frankly by this time I am feeling slightly emotional and I am unable to stop the tears coming.

G's bus is waiting when we get home so unfortunately we have an audience for H whacking his knees and head down on the ground, more grabbing at me, asking me to "clean the car" (from the drink he spilled), "help the car" (the car seat which was still miraculously attached to the seatbelt), "cuddle" etc.

G, unsurprisingly, doesn't want to come in the house initially, and tries to hurt my hand. The bus escort takes G in while I deal with H.

H wants a "pick up" so I take him to the sofa where we lie down together. He repeatedly asks for "Daddy... Marianne... Granddad's house..." - among other things.

G meanwhile is being so good... just bringing me the odd packet to open and amusing himself, bless him.

H: "Tissue... Mummy crying... Mummy sad... It's all right Mummy..." (I'm afraid that last bit made me cry more!) Then "Stroke Mummy!"

After lots of little relapses where H starts crying again he finally calms down enough to say "Ball pit... phone game."

I am then able to prise myself out from under him to get the ball pit from the shed. We put the sleeping bag ("blanket") in it and he lies down with the ipod.

It's been just over an hour since the incident started.

November 2011
Escaping G

This is getting silly. G is getting over the lovely climbable chain-link fence daily, at least once.

I have pulled any storage boxes etc away from the boundary so he can't use them as stepping stones. I have also been slowly increasing the range of obstacles to put in his path... bits of netting, chicken wire, pruned branches stuck through the existing fence, and finally a blue tarpaulin rigged across the corner of our garden going to next doors.

My garden now looks like something out of Steptoe's yard...

Have sent a letter from the occupational therapist to the landlord requesting higher fencing...

2nd November 2011
I'm pretty sure that didn't just happen...

I'm upstairs getting dressed – I will be taking H to school in a few minutes. Suddenly I hear crying.

H comes upstairs in tears asking for a cuddle. I ask him what's the matter but get no response. After a few minutes he says "Mummy hurt... red... school..."

I'm pretty sure he is remembering the incident in the car on the way home from school where he made me bleed, hence the "red".

He is distraught as if it has just happened.

Me: "Mummy is fine, look, Mummy is happy, Mummy's not hurt."

It takes a few more minutes of cuddles etc before calming down, but he is a little bit on tenterhooks until we are safely in the car on the way to school.

6th November 2011
Making your own respite

Sometimes you are lucky enough to find a place where the staff are so welcoming and accepting of your family's little foibles: the local playbarn is one such place, where some of the staff have become friends to us.

Location: The local indoor playbarn.

I think I like coming here almost as much as the boys. (Probably not as much as H, but I'm sure it's a close run thing!) Sad as it may sound, the chance to sit with books and puzzles etc, along with a nice cuppa and a cake is a real treat.

I have to be careful not to be lulled into a false sense of security though: G periodically does the rounds of the tables looking for drinks and cake to steal. (Good thing he has a strong immune system – who knows what germs he might pick up?!) H can also get a little over zealous chucking play balls around in the under 2's area... "Don't throw balls at the baby...!"

Other play areas aren't so good for us, but this one you can generally have a good view of when the kids come out of the play area.

Of course Daddy is on call to clamber around the netting and race G down the big slide, although strangely enough he won't be going down the tight turning, high speed helter-skelter head first again in a hurry!

I tell Steve this is like our version of a lazy Sunday reading the papers. Naturally it's not cheap: the entry fee, plus factor in replacement drinks that G has stolen, the inevitable C - H – I – P - S for H and of course tea and cake for us! I say who cares? It's money well spent in my book.

At this time, with the boys at this age, it feels like a real break – a small slice of "normal" family life.

6th November 2011
Deterioration of bedtime routine

Aarrgh!! What went wrong?!

H has been pants at coming into my bed in the night for the last 4 years, but he always used to have a fab going to bed routine: "Book, clean teeth first, bed, music on, night-night, I love you..." He would always go to sleep in his own bed at least.
Increasingly for the last week or so he has been quite fussy about me leaving him: "Mummy having a sleep upstairs!"
Me: "Mummy's not having a sleep yet... time for H to go to sleep!"
He then asks me for "cuddle..." etc.

Tonight he really stepped up a gear, wanting to lie down in my bed. When I pulled him out he insisted on having 'bed-cat' - the heavy draft-excluder which I put in the middle of my bed to keep him away from me a bit. So I get bed-cat to put in his bed... hmm not happy at this.
Cue crying, repeatedly grabbing me for a "cuddle" etc. He is really doing my head in now, I end up shouting "Yes, cuddle!!" into the duvet. Well you've gotta have a pressure valve somewhere.
Next I hear: "Radio on!" Very crafty, as the radio is in my bedroom. I get the radio from the bathroom and put it on. Ok he's still not happy but I eventually manage to get away.
Am feeling a little twitchy myself now so after some down time faffing around on the internet I sit down in front of the telly with a big bag of honeycomb clusters...

Correlation between mood and food...
Hmm...

7th November 2011
H's "joke"

Just woken up, stretching and yawning... ok so I was a bit 'windy' !!! I know, shocking - but I never said I was a lady!
H puts his fingers in his ears.

Then, with a big grin: "A note... it makes music!!"
Yes, very funny.

7th November 2011
Broken DVD player... (cue 'Jaws' music...)

Monday morning: H has had an anxiety attack again: his portable DVD player was not working last night so I've hidden it in a drawer. When asked for "disk" I put the disk in the main DVD player attached to the telly. H is ok with this for a few minutes then demands 2 other disks in quick succession, each time saying "disk upstairs" (where he has it at night.)

Me: DVD player broken, disk on telly."
H obviously stressed by this: "Cuddle!" This scene is repeated several times.
Then: "Help the cereal bar." (A bit was knocked off his plate during one of his mini paddies.)
Me: "We're going to school – new nappy."
H: "Cuddle!" He repeats this every few seconds, unwilling to let me go in-between times and keeps gripping me around the neck and yanking me down to him.
Manage to get nappy on then whizz away to the phone to tell school we'll be late.
I leave a message while H is once again clamped to my neck ... "Cuddle!!"
H: "Mummy red chair, (the dining room chair) Mummy having a sleep."
Honestly sometimes I think that boy doesn't know where he stops and I begin... when he's stressed or tired... "Mummy having a sleep: glasses off!"
I daren't not comply with this as we are due to go in the car soon: remember "Meltdown in the car" ?!!
We sit for a moment with glasses off. I'm getting more grumpy by the second.
Eventually get him dressed: it's "fashion day" at school so he's wearing a different top.
H: "School jumper on!"

Ok whatever, stick school jumper on.

We set off in the car. Everything is ok for a while. We are nearing school.

H: "H unhappy." Strangely he has a big smile on his face while he says this.

Me: "H was unhappy, you're happy now, H's smiling."

He stops smiling immediately I've said this – oh well.

Arriving at school: "Cuddle, pick up, Mummy pick up!" I carry him for a few steps. This isn't really by choice, he has a death grip around my neck. Suddenly he is laughing again, yelling out the name of his Teaching Assistant.

All is fine again, we go in.

Annoyingly after I get out of school I come over all emotional... what's that all about?! Sitting in the car I cannot stop the overflow, but half a dozen tears later I feel I am ok.

Oh well, have got a parent support group to go to. I'm fine, until I go in: "How are you... I'm ok... yada yada..." until the other (too perceptive) parent says that sounds like a lie...!! I Suddenly realize she is right and make my excuses for not being good company before I leg it.

My friend comes after me in the midst of my hysterical sobbing session, and a hug and a couple of jokey comments later I am ready to go back in. The wonders of a friendly word!

Funny how what has become all too much of a daily routine can grind you down, slowly, bit by bit, until you, just... Snap!!!

Cue manic laughter...

7th November 2011
Clocks going back

Good grief, third entry today!

It's H again. (Who else?! Sorry H, I do love you!)

Arriving home from school just before 4pm H says "Having a sleep, upstairs!" I try to joke a way out of it. That sometimes works with an extra cheery voice: "It's not time to sleep yet! We've just got home from school!"

He gets rather agitated by this but nothing I can't handle.

Of course now it is pitch black by 5pm.

Later on, H says: "Yogurt!" Yogurt always comes just before book, then bed.

Again I say we need tea-time first, so have got out of an extremely early bedtime. Don't get me wrong there's nothing I would like more than an occasional H-free evening but I don't fancy the 2am breakfast that may follow.

7th November 2011
G's foot fetish

For some time G has had a thing about my feet. He will kneel down on the floor where I'm sat and pull my feet into his tummy, taking my socks off.

He used to sit on one end of the sofa, leading me by the hand to sit at the other end and pull my feet up to his tummy that way. About a year ago he went through a phase of being quite insistent at pulling my feet against him... except it was lower than his tummy (yikes!!) and rocking against them, rather too firmly for my liking... Thankfully he is still in nappies - never thought I'd be thankful for that! But of course I felt rather uncomfortable at this so would get up and walk away. He soon stopped this though and went back to just wanting to curl his body up around my feet, alternately pulling my feet up into his tummy, then pushing them down again to each side of his body.

Today he was sat on the floor again with my feet by his belly. I picked up my socks, at which point he grabbed them off me, gave me a look that said "Don't even think about putting them back on!" and slung them away behind him. G doesn't need words!!

Lately he has taken to rubbing his face against the soles of my feet, say if I've been kneeling down for instance. Don't know if he's smelling them (ew!!) or just likes the feel of the exceedingly hard skin!!

Lately again, on and off for the last couple of weeks he has started trying to hump my feet again; alternately trying to pull my feet there then pushing his own hands hard against his groin.

Maybe he is starting to get sensations here? He is 10 now after all?

8th November 2011
H slept through the night!!!

I can count on the fingers of one hand the nights H has slept through in his own bed since December 2007. I mentioned in Chapter 1 how he started coming into our bed when we were away at Steve's parents, and yes, we had been many times before. Hoped it would stop when we got back home but it just carried on.

Tried the old rapid return routine, sadly this brought out the Tasmanian Devil in H: screaming, thrashing about, head spinning 360 degrees – ok maybe that last bit's an exaggeration...! Not so good when you don't want to rudely awake your other autistic child.

For a year or so we could just wait until he had flomped down on our bed; after a few minutes he would be asleep and you could take him back. The length of the periods between doing this got shorter and shorter, and each time you did it he was more and more alert. If he asked for "radio on" you knew he was a bit too awake. Radio would be turned on the absolute lowest volume setting (I have ear plugs in anyway) and we would hopefully go back to sleep. Steve is away during the week but when he is back at weekends I take my chances with sleeping under G's bed to escape the activity. Unfortunately G periodically wakes at 2am and decides it's morning, and H still comes looking for me when he gets up for good so there's not exactly a lie-in there. Was totally desperate one weekend so went and stayed at a friend's house where neither of the boys could find me: bliss!
Anyway I digress.

Other things we've tried to keep H in bed: music on repeat throughout the night, lights on, lights off, teddy in the bed, bed-cat (that heavy draught excluder!) in the bed, hot water bottle, DVD playing really quietly...

So here we are, I'm slightly demoralized by the fact I never get the bed to myself, and can no longer share a bed with my husband. (The bed's not big enough for three of us!) The night before was hideous as he didn't even want to start off in his own bed, and suddenly he goes through the night!

Shame my insomnia was striking the night before so I only got about five hours... who am I kidding... it's FIVE HOURS!!!
Woke up in the morning and had to think "what's missing here...?"
He'd had his animated alphabet DVD on the night before. When I got up I could hear it playing alongside H chuntering away to himself. I went in to find him lying in bed as Annie had left him the night before. Praised him excessively in an extremely over the top fashion: "Good boy H for staying in H's bed!" etc.

I'm sure tonight will be business as usual, but for now, it's a lovely dream!

8th November 2011
Mountain goat child

H is stood with his legs locked together so his trousers stay up above his knees, whilst holding his jumper up to his chest, baring his belly. This is the position of choice for downloading into his nappy.
"H need new nappy."
OK.
After dealing with this I go to check on G. He is stood on top of the shed, the one that says "fragile roof."

Thankfully I have a volunteer coming in the next few minutes who G loves to bounce with, so I know when he arrives G will come down. Have called my neighbour several times before, so that we could go one each side of him on a ladder and do a pincer movement.

9th November 2011
One Day

From time to time as a reference I like to jot down an entire day's events, as much as I am able. Just for comparison.
This was one such day.

5.20am
Woken by high pitched squeaking and the landing light going on: G

is up. I quickly nip to the loo only to find G has nicked the loo roll - yikes!! Never mind there's enough shredded paper from his antics left on the floor for me to use. I lock the bathroom then go back to bed. Took a sleeping tablet last night so still tired really.

5.30am

H comes in. This is actually amazing because he wasn't in my bed already! He's usually in with me by 1am. He kind of settles down.

6.30am

H is increasingly wriggly, saying "Radio on," "Mummy having a sleep" etc (clearly I'm not.) G appears and gets onto the bed with us. Danger time!

"H sitting G!" This means he is actually sitting on G.

Me: "Downstairs!"

8am

G's bus comes. He is more than ready as he has been systematically opening all the kitchen cupboard doors where he thinks I hide the back door key.

8.30am

H and I are ready to set off to school. Suddenly he spies one of Steve's big jumpers and puts it over his head, ghost style.

"H... Daddy... having a sleep Daddy!"

He refuses to let go of it and waddles out to the car. He keeps it draped over his head like a blanket all the way to school.

9.30am

No meetings today, instead I meet a friend for coffee and a natter.

1pm

Back home I am knackered, so go for a lie down. The times where I can actually go to sleep in the day are now few and far between. Instead I lay there and finish my book. Strangely after years of interrupted sleep I now find it very difficult to switch off, insomnia rules.

3.20pm

Have picked H up from school. Sadly I didn't notice that there was a puddle at the back of the car. I steer H around it but it's no good, the feet are desperately flailing to get in the puddle. We spend a few minutes with me trying to stop him slumping to the muddy ground – he might want to take his trousers off if they get dirty. H refuses to come away from the puddle and starts kicking me instead of the water.

Me: "Don't kick me."

He goes back to the puddle, splashes some more then: "Mummy clean trousers!" He means mine where he kicked me. I get out a tissue and go through the motions of wiping it clean. I bribe him with "Home, then Phil's coming to play" to get him in the car. Phil is a volunteer who comes for an hour a week to help with the boys. After a few death-grip cuddles I can get in the driver's seat. He has his fingers in his ears: "Mummy having a sleep."

I agree with him, close my eyes and take my glasses off for a moment. More cuddles are requested, this time I can just reach my hand around and tickle his cheeks, saying "cheeky cheeks!" I know what you're thinking, I'm pandering etc but I've been here before and doing all this resolves the situation so I can drive home safely. (Again: see "Meltdown in the car"!)

4.35pm

I am very lucky in that while Steve is working away SSAFA volunteers have periodically helped me out. Phil is one of them. Sadly today he hasn't come yet so I'm guessing he won't turn up.

H with a big grin: "Phil's at the door!"

Me: "Phil's not at the door yet!" (Extra jolly voice, trying not to hyperventilate here...)

Thankfully H accepts this and wanders off again.

4.45pm

Sitting at the computer perusing the internet and playing the odd game while H is watching his disk. Have been trading big squeezy hugs with a very giggly G on my knee. He very rarely puts his arms around me but he has today. I am rocking him forward then back, squeezing him tight with my arms wrapped right round him: he is laughing fit to bust – very infectious!! Mustn't get too used to this as it's a bit addictive; usually have to grab stealth cuddles while I tickle him!

5.15pm
A friend pops up online offering to come take the boys for a walk as my PA Annie isn't coming this evening. I have been so lucky in this life with the friends I have. Have just put bits on to cook for the boys when Phil turns up after all! No need for H to get upset about "Surprise... no Phil today!"

6pm
My friend has come to take the boys out just as Phil leaves, this is a real treat, one I didn't expect today! They are off to the local library, the librarian is G-proofing it in readiness. The boys are well known to my friends. G, along with his escaping tendencies has a penchant for shredding long leaved plants, so they have to be hidden, along with glue sticks and any tubes or creams etc.

Once they've toddled off I cook myself some dinner and sit down in front of the telly, it's lovely to have the house to myself for a bit. After my tea I sit and type some stuff in what Steve calls my 'blog', though it's not posted online or anything. I started it as a record of what happens in certain "incidents" and has now become some sort of therapy for me!

7.30pm
They're back! H lies down at the bottom of the stairs and refuses to take his own shoes off.
He's really knackered and says "Goodnight H!"
Soon perks up though: "Phone game!"

7.45pm
G puts the kitchen tap on full blast – water everywhere. I get him out and lock the kitchen door. G is not happy at this: repeatedly grinds his chin into the back of my hand. It's quite painful actually.

8pm
Change nappies and get them both into pyjamas. Go to put some

dirty clothes in the washing machine when I hear H giggling. This is worrying. Go back in the room and G is laying on the floor with H sitting on his head.

Me: "H off G!!"

H: "H climbing up G!"

Great.

G is fixating on an elastic band twiddling it in his fingers and squealing a lot.

H seems to think it is his duty to rip it from his fingers. A close-knit tug-o-war ensues, G gently gives H a warning headbutt. Danger, danger!! Got to stop it from all kicking off here!

Me: "G's toy, H's toy is the phone game."

H backs off, but then insists I cuddle G.

H: "Poor G!"

I have to cuddle G to placate H, meanwhile G is continuing to gouge my hand. Never mind.

8.45pm

Take H to bed. Get into my pyjamas remembering to empty my trouser pockets of the objects of G's desire that I have stashed there for safe keeping. Not too bad today: a rubber band, some effervescent vitamin C tablets and the back door key.

8.50pm

H has just got in bed when he comes down again asking for a new nappy. I sort it out and go to take him back up when I spy a Vaseline pot lid lying on the floor, with the pot nowhere to be seen. Oh dear. I take H back upstairs noting the rather greasy handrail. Lovely.

Back downstairs G is starting to chill out a little – he has been quite full of it this evening, I'm guessing because of the 2 hour sleep at school this morning.

9pm

G has calmed down a lot. Would normally have given melatonin by now but because of the sleep am worried about going too soon and him powering through the meds, or too late and he gets overtired and gets a second wind anyway!

It's the melatonin roulette game folks!

Am also worried he's not eaten nearly enough as he's been too hyper... hope he doesn't wake up at 2am but I've a nasty feeling he will be hungry in the night!!

9.20pm
G has been curled around my feet for 10 minutes; when prompted he takes himself up to bed. Yippee! Got the timing right so I didn't have to carry him up!

9.45pm
Oh crap. Heard coughing upstairs so went to check. H has spewed everywhere! Bizarrely he stays pretty much asleep while I manhandle him out of his PJs, swap pillows and sling another sheet over the bed and change the duvet cover.
If he needs to sleep now will bath him in the morning. He rouses himself enough to request a different DVD but is asleep again before I have even changed disks.

Have to say the sick part is not a usual occurrence! I have a sneaking suspicion that H was minesweeping G's plate earlier and G's vaseline-y fingers may have left some on the food... aaargh!!

10.30pm
Have been looking around for the missing vaseline to no avail – am hoping it doesn't make an unwelcome reappearance in G's hands in the middle of the night.

10.40pm
Stick all the sicky washing on.

10.50pm
Sit down with a cuppa and an American cop series. I've been looking forward to this!

11.55pm
Off to bed now. Usually read for a bit to switch off but am going to try a couple of puzzles and listen to some tunes on the ipod tonight instead. Hope I get to sleep soon!

12 midnight

More sick from H. He is barely awake again:

"H cold!" His PJ's are all cold and wet from his exploits. Grab another change of clothes. The bath is now full of stuff waiting to be washed in the morning. Am scouting around for any old towels or sheets etc I can chuck on H's bed again. Fingers crossed I don't make too much racket and wake G!

3am-ish

Don't really know what time it is now as H is sick again, though I don't reckon he's got much left inside him!

5.30am

H gets up and comes into my bed. I quickly grab a couple more towels to spread over my bed – just in case!

"Cuddle!" I have to lie on my side with my arm over him which he has in a death grip. Unfortunately this is an impossible sleep position for me.

Oh well, roll on bedtime tonight!

Chapter 3

Fun times

We are still house hunting here and Steve will be out of the RAF in just over a year. My insomnia is pretty bad these days, I find it really hard to switch off and go to bed straight away after the boys have gone; I like that little bit of evening to myself! I also then have to read or do puzzles for ages in bed until I can't keep my eyes open any longer. It's my own stupid fault I know. I often then wake up after not very long at all with palpitations. I was slightly alarmed by this but on speaking to a psycho-therapist friend I'm apparently having more REM sleep and less deep sleep as I have lots of stress to get out. Well, maybe!

13th November 2011
"H sad!"

The last week or so, especially since he was ill, H has been on an emotional swingometer!
Will be fine one minute, then giggling or smiling: "H unhappy!"
Me: "H's not unhappy, you're smiling!"
Today I was watching the last post playing at the cenotaph as it is Remembrance Sunday.
H: "That's not the Gigglebiz, Mummy get Gigglebiz!" (Gigglebiz is a children's TV programme.)

He comes over for a cuddle. He is very grippy and cuddly at this point.

I put Gigglebiz back on.

"H unhappy." (Kind of smiling though...) Then:

"H sad!" (No smiling this time.)

A bout of crying ensues, H repeatedly telling me he is sad.

13th November 2011
Angry G

It's not been easy, the whole thing where Steve is just here for weekends. Unfortunately some weekends he has to go back to work even earlier on a Sunday, as he then has to travel on elsewhere.

2pm

I pick G up from the carer's. He hasn't seen Steve all weekend and Steve has to leave at 3pm so he spends a lot of time bouncing with G.

Marianne (Annie) "comes to play" and help with the boys.

Just before Steve leaves we realise G has got into the neighbour's garden. Steve goes and brings him back. G goes back into our garden. Steve leaves.

A little while later the rest of us go out in the car, stopping off at a local playground.

Both boys are happy here, G is particularly full of glee.

Around 4.30pm it gets rather chilly so we go off to McDonalds for tea.

On the way there G starts playing with the electric windows, constantly putting them down and sticking his hands out.

5 pm: McDonalds

All is fine for around half an hour while we eat. G nibbles a few chicken nuggets. He has a helium balloon on a ribbon to play with. He is quite bouncy, standing up on the seat in the booth twiddling with the ribbon. He soon starts trying to get past Annie sitting in the booth. He then suddenly picks up the drink bottle and throws it past Annie onto the floor. Annie picks up the bottle and puts it in the bag. G then "asks" for the bottle so Annie gives it back to him thinking he wants a drink.

This time he really chucks it.

After a final trip to the loo we go back to the car.

Annie straps G in his seat and shuts the door. G promptly opens the door and chucks out his shoes.

Fast-forward: we are driving home. G is fiddling with the windows again. It's quite distracting trying to override him putting the windows down with the driver's side control whilst being very aware of a large set of headlights close in my rear-view mirror.

We turn off the dual carriageway.

G hits the indicator switch.

I turn the indicator off.

G gouges my hand. He then turns on the hazard lights.

I turn them off.

G gouges my hand again.

H is getting upset: "Mummy's hurt!"

G opens the car door.

Yikes!! Stop!!!

This time it's me who turns the hazards on!

I ask Annie to move into the middle of the back seat so I can put G's seat behind my chair.

Annie holds onto G's reins to stop G from following me into the road while I move his chair.

G gouges me some more.

I put him into his seat and we continue home safely – while G constantly rocks towards Annie, growling at her and trying desperately to open the back door despite the child lock.

Once we are home G goes into the garden, but is obviously still very angry. Every few minutes Annie goes to check on him only to have G growl at her.

One of the times we find him fiddling with the stepladder, probably planning his escape route.

He spends the best part of the next hour on the trampoline.

7.50pm

G comes in and sits down to eat. Think we're ok now.

15th November 2011
Verbalizing while upset

Latest verbal spout from H, after a H and G upset: "G broken... red light... stuck... telly sleep..." (whilst bashing the telly) then quite strangely: "Telly have new nappy..."

18th November 2011
Friday: "Daddy's coming to play!"

Aargh!! Aargh!!! Told H Daddy was coming to play at 8 o'clock... now I'm getting "Help the 8 o'clock!!"
Unfortunately just moving the clock hands won't make us time travel...

21st November 2011
Monday night is zopiclone night! (Other sleeping pills *are* available.)

3.45am: G is up, giggling fit to bust, and I've taken a zopiclone sleeping tablet. Oh joy!
Trashed the next day doesn't come close to covering it!

21st November 2011
"Phone game flag"

H has an ipod touch loaded with simple games etc. It has a black cover; this is the "black phone game". Steve also has an ipod with a lot of the same games on it, plus some music videos and podcasts. It has a Union Jack cover; this is the "phone game flag".

H has lately been asking for the "phone game flag".
Last night as Steve left for work, as well as saying goodbye to Daddy I made H say goodbye to the phone game flag. You might think that this would work... you would be wrong.
This morning: "Phone game flag!"

Me: "Phone game flag with Daddy, black phone game!" (Offering the alternative here.)
H: "Phone game flag!!!"
Me: "Daddy has phone game flag, 4 sleeps, then phone game flag."
Crying, gripping around the legs, yelling "pick up!" etc, soon escalates to screaming as I go upstairs to get some socks for G.

Meanwhile G's bus has arrived. I've come downstairs to gather his things together.
Bus lady: "Quick, H's coming over the banisters!"
Shit!! I quickly go upstairs, shouting "H down" and "danger!"
Deciding that the ground floor is probably a better place to have this 'conversation' I get H downstairs. This consists of me going down slowly backwards in front of H: trying to lift up his sprawling writhing body whilst preventing him from bouncing his head off every step, yelling; "Whoops!"
G beats a hasty exit with the bus lady. Lots of "Cuddle... Mummy sleep... glasses off... H sad..." takes up the next half an hour.

Have been house hunting... a bungalow is now very high on my wish list.

22nd November 2011
Bad timing?

8.55pm
G has had his melatonin, he's been getting up quite early and had a sleep at school this morning.

9.25pm
Goes up to bed, turns his bedroom light on and shuts the door.

9.55pm
I sneak in, all is quiet so I turn out the light.

10pm
G comes downstairs again, I change his nappy. 10 minutes or so later I take him back upstairs.

11pm

G appears to be asleep.

This really could have been so much worse.

23rd November 2011

Communication

H has a scab on his wrist from a friction burn off a slide. This happened 3 days ago.

H has noticed it again.

"Hurt!"

"H's not hurt, it's all better."

Tries to bite the scab: "Eat... red... hurt... YES!!"

25th November 2011

Planning for the week... success!

Years ago living in Germany I made some good friends. For the last few years we have tried (not always successfully!) to get together once a year for what has become affectionately termed "Girly weekend."

Our lives had become quite different since we were last together and I was worried at first about having nothing to talk about; or worse, becoming an autism bore! I shouldn't have worried. Lifelong friends are lifelong friends!

On Tuesday morning I introduced H to a simple written timetable for the week, to prepare him for me being away for "2 sleeps." I wrote the day and date at the top of each day, said "Today is Tuesday 22, Monday 21 finished." Then read through each day: school, Marianne etc. H straightaway skipped through to the day where G goes to his carer's house, then lost interest.

Each morning progressed fine, saying the day before was finished, and crossing through with a marker pen.

This morning at school I said:

"School, then Mummy goes out for 2 sleeps."

H was fine with this and didn't appear worried that I wasn't around: the weekend went without a hitch!

26th November 2011
Cuddling strange children

On my weekend away with my old girlfriends Steve takes H on the train to Ely as G is at the carer's.

Steve and H are enjoying a coffee in Costa (well Steve is) when a woman comes in with a crying baby in a pushchair.
Quick as a flash H nips over and cuddles the child. Child stops crying abruptly.
Thankfully the woman (and everyone else in Costa) thinks this is amusing.

In 10 years time not so sure this would go down as well.
Must work on the personal space thing.

27th November 2011
Apologize nicely

Steve and Annie have taken the boys to the soft play barn while I am away.
H likes to collect a couple of plastic play balls at a time and then climb up to the top of the slide so he can roll them down.
Another child keeps pinching the balls.
H hits the child.
"H you don't hit other children: what do you say?"
H: "Sorry children."

27th November 2011
"It's not you, it's me..."

Ok so I am back from my weekend away.
After some lovely welcome home cuddles with H he pipes up: "Phone game flag!" He hasn't asked Steve or Annie for this at all, all weekend. It is after all Steve's phone game, not mine?!

Also a few months back a friend looked after H while Steve and I were house-hunting. She walked him around several different shops, with him never once asking "We're going... we're going...?" As soon as I collect him and put him back in our car... "We're going?"

Am so glad the constant annoying requests are just saved for Mummy...

5th December 2011
Normal kind of morning

3am (ish)
H has helped himself to the lion's share of my bed. Bed-cat the draught excluder no longer goes down the middle of my bed as H demands it goes in his at bedtime. I attempt to lump H over to the far side of the bed. Fail miserably.

Note to self: get another draught excluder.

6am
Have got rather a crick in the neck as I have been lying on my side on the edge of the bed for the last 3 hours instead of my habitual face down pose.

7am
Am pretty desperate for the loo now as I've been awake a while. Attempt to sneak out of bed without waking the wee one but again fail.

"Mummy stretch! (I oblige.) Mummy get downstairs."

Off we go. We have a new visual timetable on which I point out the morning's activities to H.

7.40 am
H: "Sticker on the hand!" What? Why?! I get a plaster out and we wrap it around his thumb. Ok. He's slightly agitated now. Cuddle.

Me: "H have cereal bar for breakfast."

H: "Grapes, no cereal bar... cereal bar sleep!"

Ooookay.

I get a couple of grapes, then H asks for the cereal bar he's just spurned, then an orange.

It's slow going but eventually we get through breakfast.

7.50am

Manhandle G around his bed into a new nappy and then his clothes while he's still half asleep. Carry him downstairs complete with a rather large stuffed sheep that he won't release from his clutches.

I really would like a bungalow.

5th December 2011
Had to stop on the way home again today

H: "Computer... CBeebies... Home... Mummy..."
Me: "Yes CBeebies on the computer at home."
H: "Mummy..."
Me: "Yes H."
H: "Mummy, Mummy Mummy!"
Me: " Oh... Mummy!"
I'm afraid my correct rendition of the required repetition is too late though...
"Cuddle..."

Oh no.

Me: "Mummy stop the car, then cuddle, stop the car first, then cuddle. I have to find a safe place to stop the car... (aaargh!!) Mummy stop the car at the white house." (This is a pub on the main road.)
I pull in to the car park, give H a cuddle etc. H gets out of the car.
Me: "Where are you going?!"
H: "White house!" I have a wrist in each hand here, we are right next to the main road!
Me: "White house closed."
H: "White house open...!"

Well, you get the picture here.
A bit more yelling, pulling hair (mine, not his) and cuddling and we are able to get safely back into the car and resume our journey.
I don't know why these things have to happen when you are desperate to get home to the loo.

5th December 2011
Bedtime

9pm
G has his melatonin.

11.50pm
Still lots of stomping around in his bedroom making the rocking chair bang against the radiator etc.

Midnight
He's downstairs again. I really need to go to bed now. Have been up so long waiting for him to settle I have eaten a whole bag of Galaxy Counters and feel slightly sick.

12.05am
He is now running around the lounge batting a balloon about.

12.10am
Time to change his nappy again.

12.30am
Yep, still up.

12.40am
Finally, he's asleep! My eyes are burning. Am seriously thinking of leaving him on the sofa rather than lug him up into his bed. But then H will be down early with me and will go for trampolining practice on G's back. Hmm maybe not...

8th December 2011
Hide and seek

Things I have hidden in my knicker drawer to keep G from trying to eat them: marshmallows, chewy sweets, deodorant, perfume, lavender pillow spray, menthol, a pink glittery eraser bought as a present for my niece 2 years ago, ear plugs.
Yes, I do have knickers in there too.

9th December 2011
Still escaping

It's Friday evening and G is going to the carer's for the night. I am grilling sausages and preparing a bag of food and clothes to take with him while he bounces on the trampoline outside.
I am checking him every few minutes.

Obviously not often enough.
He has hotfooted it over the fence at the back and is skipping around the garden next door to the one that backs onto us.
Time to knock up my neighbour again to sit with H while I go on a retrieval exercise.

Still no sign of any extra fencing from the landlord in response to the Occupational Therapist's letter.

10th December 2011
McDonalds

We are in H's favourite café: G quite likes it too as he can eat all the batter off the chicken nuggets. Then I can thriftily pass the middle bits over to H.
Waste not want not.

We are in one of the booths in McDonalds, the idea is that the kids are wedged in their places.
Not so. G slips by behind Steve, running over the top of the chair back.
I leap up and head him off as he sprints a circuit around the shop, asking Steve to get the reins we have left in the car. Yep, that was sensible!
Meanwhile H has to copy everything G does and is gleefully running around after him.

We settle down to eat again (indigestion!) and put the reins on G. Unfortunately he slips by behind Steve again – he is fast – and sits down next to a couple of old gentlemen at another table. I apologise and drag G away from the table only to have him curl up in a ball on the floor. He seems to have a knack of making himself an immovable object; he actually seems heavier than he is, and with elbows tucked in so I can get no purchase on him it's like trying to lift a concrete block! I proceed to shuffle him along the floor with my feet much to the amusement of a nearby family.

I ask Steve to please hook his arm through the reins this time (note the gritted teeth).

All settles down as we finally get back to our table. The little girl at the next table is asking her Mummy why G is wearing reins. Mummy says she doesn't know.

Are you kidding? After that performance?!

We finish up, deciding that H has had enough chips. Steve takes G back to the car. Meanwhile I give H two more chips and hide the rest in the rubbish. The little sauce tub is nearly empty: "More sauce!"

I scrape the last two chips around the tub getting up plenty of sauce but H can't cope with the fact that the bottom of the tub is showing. He has a mini-meltdown, grabbing me around the neck, yanking my hair, and re-visiting the traumatic time of "Mummy hurt nose!" I have to take my glasses off, pretend to sleep, then "cuddle the nose" (H does this by putting his face next to mine). He is flailing about a little, insists on smacking the glass window which he then pulls my head towards to make me "cuddle" it.

At this point I catch the eye of the woman at the next table who is wondering what the hell is going on. I give her a grin: "Autism... don't you just love it!" Not sure she's seeing the funny side.

After going through the required rituals H calms down and gets a bit giggly. We are just getting up to go when H swoops down on the next table's dinner and nicks a chicken nugget. Ok quite embarrassed now. More apologies, they assure me it's ok. We exit the building, I notice the woman as we walk past the window studiously avoiding eye contact.

Oops.

16th December 2011
Keep on moving...

6.20 am: Fidget times 10

I am really tired and still trying to get some rest in bed. H is awake.
He is nattering on about different days and dates, what might be happening. Part of the ritual is that I have to repeat it back to him.
I am mumbling and slurring: "Sunday 1 school?! No school on a Sunday... H being funny..." Zzz

Meanwhile...
More turning over, moving around, constantly kneeling on my hair as he strains to get even closer to me: don't think this is actually possible! Putting his fingers on my face, pulling at my eyelids to open my eyes saying "Eyes on!" Pressing my nose, lying across my body dangling head down off the edge of the bed, using my legs as a slide when I bring my knees up...

An hour later we are downstairs and H is tucked up on the sofa playing the phone game. Laying there quite still.
Really.
Just still.

19th December 2011
Bedtime

G has one of those beds that has steps up and a slide down. It's handy because when Steve is home I can go and sleep on the mattress underneath G's bed and hopefully enjoy a H-less night.
The plan is when we move this year we will have a 4 bed house so we can divert G back to a simple divan bed. I remind myself of this every time he goes to sleep on the sofa downstairs and I have to hump his dead weight upstairs and up and over the lip of his raised bed. "Only a few more months...!"

I'm hoping that this time-scale will still hold as lately G has been going to bed, chucking the mattress out of the way and bouncing on the wooden slats.

Not sure how long the bed is going to last...
On the plus side there really is no point now in making his bed.

20th December 2011
Memory

The bin lorry is outside emptying the wheelie bins. H comes out to watch.
"Bubble toy broken... bubble toy gone."
It has been some time now since H had a wobbly, threw down his bubble toy and broke it, upon which I put it in the bin to show it had gone. A few weeks after this incident he wanted the bubble toy and insisted on going through the bin to try and find it.
Hopefully now he has seen the bins being emptied this will address the matter!

23rd December 2011
"Christmas Day"

I don't think H has got the concept of holidays: "Car to the Christmas Day!"
No amount of "25 December is Christmas Day" is working...
I feel an impromptu trip to the house bedecked with all the lights coming on, hereafter to be called "Christmas Day."

26th December 2011
update

Well we went in the "car to Christmas day" last night and very pretty and twinkly the house was too. Got out of the car, had a little look around, made H say goodbye to Christmas day and that seemed to do the trick. Next year we will stick to calling it "December 25"!!

28th December 2011
Bedtime routine: holidays

Well H's night-time routine has gone right up the swannee while we've been away.

He stays in a room with 2 single beds: H in one, Steve in the other. An extended game of bed swapping then carries on throughout the night as H subconsciously looks for body warmth. (Yes I've tried hot water bottles, teddies etc.) We decided to push the 2 single beds together with "bedcat" lying down the middle in the hope H would stay put. It seems to work. Only thing is now he won't stay in bed initially when he goes up.

He constantly keeps coming out... only goes to sleep now when Steve goes up to bed with him.

Am now rather worried what is going to happen when we get back home...

Thankfully the part where he needed someone to initially stay up in bed with him didn't persist after we got home... phew!

Chapter 4

Can anybody please send chocolate...?

There was a time when G seemed to be the more difficult one. After all, he couldn't speak, didn't use any form of signing or picture exchange communication system: he didn't even point to things. He would head butt, a lot. Scream, be up at night half the time.

So when H started saying his first words when giving me the relevant symbols ("grapes!") we thought: how wonderful!!

But as his vocabulary grew, his understanding of meaning didn't grow with it: it was like there was suddenly too much to make sense of. Trust me, the ability to speak didn't always have very much to do with communication in our house!

Whereas G: in time I came to understand him, and he could communicate with me just fine. You want to go out? Stick your shoes in my face. You want food? Drag me by the hand to the kitchen cupboard.

H, on the other hand: "Move... you want there... no... no you want there... you want no... arrgh!! Mummy yes talking!"

Yep, speech vs communication. Sometimes silence is a wonderful thing. You know the saying: be careful what you wish for...

6th January 2012
Current H "quirks"

*   Monotone humming
*   An unhealthy obsession with the "Mummy private" area...
*   Wanting to sit on my neck, and "cuddle on my neck"
*   Gets unreasonably upset by any "hurt" places, even down to a little bit of skin pulled away by my fingernail – I had to have a "sticker" (plaster) on it immediately.

8th January 2012
Ouch

My right hand is really painful again where G has been constantly grinding his chin into the back of it. He seems to have an un-erring talent for finding weak spots between the tendons...

8th January 2012
Tired inside and out

Still not got a house, so slightly stressed about that on top of everything else! We've made an offer on one but are going through having a survey done, as it is a big old damp place that probably needs loads doing to it.
We know how to pick 'em!

H is in bed, Steve has just gone back to work for the week.
Front door is wide open to listen out for H while G and I sit in the car outside the house. G is a little twitchy after Steve leaving, and this settles him.
Really emotionally drained today...

I'm sure it's quite normal to sit in silence with your boy with tears sliding down your face...

14th January 2012
Self harming

I'm trying to break H from the habit of taking my glasses off after he gets upset: "Mummy sleep, glasses off, cuddle..."
I'm making a stand on this as it can be dangerous, especially when I'm driving as previously mentioned!

Needless to say when I wouldn't comply with the "glasses off" he went off on one.
Cue lots of slapping his head, asking for "sticker", throwing himself on the ground chucking his head backwards.
"You want hurt!"
I am trying to hold his fists as he punches himself in the cheek.
Me: "Stop... don't hit yourself... don't hurt yourself... don't hurt Mummy..." etc.

It's very difficult to deal with and quite upsetting when your child wants to hurt themselves. H has made a connection between needing to be "hurt" (either himself or me, or the phone game or any other offending article) and then having a "cuddle" to make it better before the upset can be resolved.

6th January 2012
Language perception

H, on seeing a patch of frost on the ground: "Snow!"
Me: "That's not snow, that's frost; it's not as thick as snow."
H, mis-hearing "thick as" for "sticker" (a plaster): "No sticker!!"
Me: "No, no sticker, it's fine."

H, a little while after asking for CBeebies: "Golden coming... Mummy get golden coming."
Me, puzzled: "Show Mummy the golden coming."
H takes my wrist, pushing it up towards the phone, then down towards the computer. I suddenly have a lightbulb moment as to what he means... "Golden coming" is the Google Chrome tab that opens up onto Google, where H clicks on the history to get

CBeebies!
Perception of words obviously needs work, bless him.

17th January 2012
"Daddy's broken..."

H has randomly been saying "Daddy broken" on and off, kind of like a joke.
(Me: "Daddy's not broken, H's funny!")
Had another belated light-bulb moment today when H said the phone game was "broken", then "working."
H says goodbye to Daddy every Sunday night when Daddy goes to "work"... Doh!!

18th January 2012
Playing in the road... probably not a good idea...

We've just left school and are walking back to the car. There is a big puddle at the side of the road at the junction. H is suddenly possessed of the compulsion to go into the road and kick his foot through the water. Unfortunately there is a car trying to back around the corner.
Me, holding desperately onto his arm, "Not in the road, danger!!"
Lots of screaming, pulling towards the road, falling down onto the ground, etc.
I manage to get him to our car. His trousers are now wet on the knees.
H: "Trousers off, nappy off!" He proceeds to strip.
I get him into the back of the car where H is now bottomless.
"Pyjamas off!" They are not pj's but this makes sense to H. He is trying to get his top and jumper off, and is getting in a right state about it.
Finally he is naked in the back of the car. "Red trousers on!" (From his pj's.)
Me: "Home, then red trousers on." This doesn't go down well.
After a few minutes: "Pyjamas on." (Meaning clothes.)
I manage to get the same pull-up nappy back on: just as well as I

don't have a spare one in the car.

We have to put H's trousers on back to front so he can't see the offending wet bits.

Finally get going. Five minutes later I'm instructed to pull over and put on his shoes.

Note to self: need to get new shoes for him as the weakening Velcro on the straps is now a cause for distress.

A couple of minutes later we are driving again, H is still stressing.

"Seatbelt off... red trousers on... Mummy sleep... glasses off... cuddle..." etc.

Me: "Home, then seatbelt off / red trousers on / Mummy sleep / cuddle." (Please delete as applicable.)

A few minutes more. "Mummy come back!"

"I'm here, Mummy is here."

"Orange... orange, car... you want orange car."

"No orange in the car, home then orange."

A few seconds... "You want no, no orange car."

Ok, no orange car...

26th January 2012
Comforting

This was very unlike G to "say sorry" after a gouging session.

Annie was babysitting the boys while I was out. She has a plaster cast on her arm as her wrist is fractured.

G is getting a bit fretful and pulls at her arm to get her attention.

This is really pretty painful for Annie: "G... no!"

He tries to Chinese burn her other arm so she moves away.

A minute later G comes up to her and leans his head against her tummy.

She strokes his hair:

"It's all right G."

27th January 2012 8.20am
Happy Friday everyone!

Don't you just love everything going tits up on a Friday when the school run traffic is always at it's most manic anyway...!

The phone game is "not working" as H keeps managing to put it in standby mode.
Me: "H play with cars."
This could have been a brilliant distraction, except... suddenly:
"Blue lorry..."
Damn, damn, there is a trailer loose in the toy box that obviously belonged to a blue lorry. IT'S NOT THERE!!!!

"Blue lorry... blue lorry... aaargh... cuddle... lorry..."
A bit of banging himself down on the floor commences along with scraping his wrists along the carpet.
"Sticker... hurt... Mummy get sticker..."
"Sticker" is applied to the wrist, then: "You want two stickers!" The other wrist is obviously feeling left out.
"Sticker off!"
Plaster off.
"Sticker on!"
Lucky I know to stick the plaster on myself for future use, we get through a lot of plasters.
"Cuddle!!"

Me, after several aborted attempts to move on: "Mummy getting dressed."
It's 8.50am: we're supposed to be at school in 5 minutes and it's a 20 minute drive.
I quickly phone the school amid the yelling from H to give them the heads up and go upstairs to get dressed.
H is not happy at this. (Notice the subtle understatement.)

After hearing a bit of thudding and crashing and H yelling "Help!" he barrels up the stairs.
"Pick up, pick up upstairs!!"
I manage to get my bra and knickers on before picking him up for 2

seconds and then putting him down on my bed. Obviously not good enough.

He is down on the floor again and whacks his knees and head down. "Hurt head, clean the head..."

Me, rubbing his head: "Head is clean."

I finish chucking on clothes and go downstairs, followed by yelling and running feet. He catches me up two steps up from the bottom: "Pick up upstairs!!" I pick him up from the step, then put him down in the hallway.

He scoots off... "Whoops... you want whoops!" He has pulled his visual timetable off the door and all the little pictures are all over the place. He then found the phone game and slung it across the room. H carries on shouting "Whoops!" into my face until I repeat it back to him: "Yes, whoops!"

Thankfully H already has his uniform on. Starts going on about the phone game again, asking me to cuddle it, which I do. (I know, I know!)

He then gets into his normal morning position of lying on the sofa with the phone game with a blanket over him. I'm hoping we are getting close to the re-set stage where we can start afresh.

Me: "Shoes on, we're going to school."

H: "No shoes."

Hmm.

I'm pretty stressed by this time so walk away and put his bits in the car ready.

Fast forward.

We are driving to school, all I want to do now is cry.

H keeps up a running commentary of the following interspersed with my denials:

"You want cuddle... stop the car... home... Mummy sleep... no school... nappy... monkey pyjamas..."

Thankfully I have a lock of sorts over H's seatbelt, so despite repeated wanging around of his head and arms he can't get out.

Finally we get to school, all the kids have gone to assembly. As soon as one of the TA's comes back and I have to speak, that's it: I can't stop myself from crying.

Marvellous!

H seems perfectly happy now, if a little bemused.

It's been an hour since the incident started.

Felt like two.

30th January 2012
Anxiety?

Every week day morning at the moment H seems to be getting stressed over something or other.

This morning I think it was because he had a snuffly nose. It started with H asking for a nappy and making little noises that I know from experience will turn into a whine.

Me: "Mummy get new nappy." H whinges.

Me, in a cheery voice: "Hello?" (This sometimes helps stop things in their tracks.)

More whinging.

Yikes, it's not working.

He tries to scrape my wrist with his fingers, then says "Mummy sticker."

I keep telling him Mummy will get sticker downstairs, new nappy etc with him whining all the while, insisting on me carrying him.

Downstairs he drags his own wrist along the carpet, now he must have a sticker too. He gets very fractious and agitated, yelling over and over again about the "stickers" – whilst I am constantly agreeing over and over again that I am getting the sticker.

I have a bit of a moment at this point and yell: "Sticker: Mummy is getting sticker, sticker, sticker STICKER!!!"

He finally settles on the sofa with the phone game, but the blanket he has over him is obviously not behaving itself properly, and despite a lot of attempting to smooth and re-arrange it, H's legs are flailing and he is now crying in earnest.

I walk away.

10 seconds later he is after me saying "Throw phone game!" I see it on the floor, he picks it up then comes to me by the computer.

He then says: "Yellow birds... 3 flags."

I don't know what that is about... though it's probably to do with one of his games on the ipod.

I have actually just opened up a document on the computer to jot some of this down, so on a blank page I write:

Yellow birds 3 flags

It kind of stops him in his tracks while he reads it, he is almost smiling now. I then distract him by offering him an orange. This seems to work for a bit but he then gets in a state of confusion, between wanting CBeebies on the computer and sitting at the table with the orange.

"Mummy table." (He is still sat at the computer.) I sit at the table. Not the right answer... "You want stand up!!"

Right...

It eventually gets resolved by clicking a few times on the website, having a look, then he is able to go to the table himself and have the orange.

We are on heightened amber alert state for the rest of the morning until we get in the car to go to school.

6th February 2012
Inappropriate language...

First off: to my knowledge H has never walked in on my hubby and me getting "friendly" unless I was of course comatose through lack of sleep at the time.

H is rather obsessed at the moment with touching my bits. Have mentioned this to the OT, and she has devised a little game where you take pictures of body parts out of a bag and put them on the "touch" or "don't touch" sheet.

H seems to get the hang of this, we finish the game. By this time H has sat on my lap on the sofa with his phone game.

He makes what I call his "mischief noise" and tries to sneak his hand around to my bits – or Mummy's "private" as it's known to him.

Me: "Don't touch private."

H: "Private, don't touch."

Me: "That's right, don't touch private."
H: "Eating place."
Me: ???
H: "Eating place!"
Me: "Eating place??! Ew, that's not right! H's being funny!"
He laughs.

Really. In front of the Social Services OT.
And no, I have NO idea where that came from!

7th February 2012
Annie's story – double meltdown

I have gone out for the evening, singing with a choir group that's been recently formed at the RAF base. (More about the choir later. Trust me, you'll be sick of me going on about it!)
I'm having a lovely time. Meanwhile...

Bathtime: all is normal.
8pm: everything's fine.
8.10pm: H has his yogurt.
8.15pm: H has a little bit of a stress moment with the position of the sleeping bag on the sofa but soon gets over this.
8.25pm: Book, brush teeth, toilet, all good. Goes to say goodnight to G whose legs are dangling from the loft hatch in his bedroom. Aaarrgh!!

Annie gets G down, and by 8.45pm H is in bed and seems settled.
Annie is giving G his melatonin when H kicks off. She hurries to put the lid on the medicine, shuts the kitchen door, runs upstairs.
H is in the throes of a major meltdown.
He is "hurting" everything. Throwing the radio and DVD player, scraping his wrists along the floor, giving death-grip hugs to Annie so she can't breathe, etc.
35 minutes later she has managed to calm him down and he is in bed again.

Annie finally gets downstairs to find G has managed to get into the kitchen, take the lid off the medicine, and empty an entire bottle of melatonin onto the floor. (This stuff is heinously expensive!!)
G then gets angry because Annie tells him off for the second time that evening.
9.35pm G starts to settle down.

I realise after Annie has told me all this that G didn't have his respiridone this morning. Well, we were wondering what his behaviour would be like if he didn't have it!

10th February 2012
Communication

"Telly... ketchup... coming... phone game, pod."
I repeat this back to H very slowly... phone game and pod (ipod) are the same thing... not sure what the rest means.
H then says: "Not."
Hmm.
Random.

10th February 2012
Socks in the snow

G just asked for some clean socks on, and a pair of pj bottoms that are too short. 2 seconds later he is out in the snow and bouncing on the trampoline. I wonder how many pairs of socks I will find in the garden after the snow has melted...

11th February 2012
Such a proud moment...

We are in the playground by the woods. There is still snow and ice on the ramp leading up to the slide so it is too slippery for H to climb. He gets a little fretful at this, so I try and divert him.
"H climb up ladder."

He goes to the ladder, takes a step up, then says: "Fuck... fuck's sake."

Damn it. Ok I might have muttered this once, under my breath after being cut up by someone in the car... I'm only human after all!
A couple are playing with their toddler not too far away – yikes! I ignore H hoping he'll carry on climbing the ladder.
Sadly I have forgotten (how could I?!) H's obsession with making me echolalic too – he wants me to repeat it back to him. It's a very crisp cold day and his voice rings out lovely and clear as he ups the volume: "Fuck's sake...? Fuck's sake...?!?"
Aaargh!!
There's only one way out of this...
Me: "Fuck's sake? That's not a nice thing to say! We don't say those words!"

Phew! Have managed to repeat the lovely language without (I hope!) endorsing it, therefore forestalling the inevitable physical meltdown peppered by expletives.

Such a proud Mummy... oh dear...

13th February 2012
G: pushing the boundaries

I am quite used to other-worldly G, bouncing around the place with a bit of shredded loo roll in his fingers.
Now I've got a kind of hybrid G, a cross between the terrible twos and a hormonal teenager.
Increasingly trying to climb, especially into the loft hatch above his bed, then chucking stuff like lego around when I'm trying to tidy it up whilst laughing in my face.

14th February 2012
"Four toast!"

Tea time. I have done a small bowl of ravioli and two pieces of buttered toast, sandwiched and cut into triangles. It seems to be going down well. H is managing to spoon bits in slowly by himself so I pop to the kitchen.

"Toast... 4 toast..."

One slice of the toast has been eaten leaving 4 neat triangles on the plate.

"H has four pieces of toast... look: one, two, three, four."

Not the right answer. A period of trying to reason with H ensues...

"Four toast!!!"

Incoming!! Here comes the screaming, thrashing child that lurks in the background, just waiting to be awakened by some obscure rule that has been broken. (Well it's obscure to me!)

"Whoops! You want pick up!!"

The ravioli is on the floor along with H. I have to pick up the ravioli before things deteriorate further. There is now quite a high pitch of screaming.

A few more minutes pass.

He is now dragging me to the kitchen.

Me: "Show Mummy the four toast."

Dragged to the fridge, we look inside but he keeps shutting the fridge ("No!") then wants it open again. In between the opening and slamming of the fridge door I manage to grab the jar of paste. This seems ok.

I then put new bread in the toaster ("Waiting for the pop!") and spread the paste on it when it's done. This also seems ok.

I cut it into squares as this is how I normally do his paste on toast.

"Triangle!"

I refuse to do a third lot of toast so cut the squares into little triangles so it looks like a union jack.

This seems to do the trick.

Although H will happily eat buttered toast or toast with jam on at breakfast time, obviously the only kind of toast we can have at tea-time is paste.

Since this incident I have kept to cutting the toast into triangles.

22nd February 2012
Night time play

4.07am
G comes into my bedroom. He is wandering in and out randomly, turning the light on and off, then curling up on the end of my bed.

4.30am
H comes in to my bed next to me, but is quite fidgety as G is down by his feet and keeps wriggling about.

4.35am
G flicks the room light switch on and off about 8 times really quickly, runs back to my side of the bed and jumps over my legs – he's quite good at missing me. Meanwhile H has got up and turned the light off again, then whizzed after G, scrambling over my legs – he's not so good at leaving me bruise-free.

5am: They have been whizzing round and round after each other, whacking lights on and off and cackling hilariously. Things finally settle down a little and G takes himself back into his room. Unfortunately H is wide awake now so it's time to get up.

25th February 2012
Learning new words

So Steve took the boys out for a drive this evening and hit a deer as it ran into the road. Now H "Echolalia boy" has learnt lots of lovely new words from Daddy!!
Just hope he doesn't repeat them in company...

29th February 2012
Speech / Hearing perception?

H and I are listening to the radio in the car, The Jam "That's Entertainment" is playing.

H: "Munnan."

Huh?

Again: "Munnan!"

Me: "Munnan?"

"It's your rennant munnan."

Quickly catching on here: "Rennant munnan? They are saying 'that's entertainment.'"

Don't care to be corrected, thanks - getting a bit stressed now.

"It's your rennant munnan!"

I repeat this as I know this is what he wants. Still not good enough though.

"It's your rennant munnan!!"

I have to repeat this a couple more times before my inflection meets H's approval.

I don't know if this is an issue with the way he perceives sounds, but I'm often required to repeat things back in a precise way, that doesn't bear any resemblance to what I have actually heard. Doesn't matter if it's spoken words from the radio or telly, or words from a song. He still seems to hear things differently from the way I do.

4th March 2012
Spitting

9.30 pm

Well my lovely first-born got back from the carer's tonight and has been spitting gleefully on the floor (mostly the kitchen lino thank goodness!) for the last hour and a half. Just ignore it, just ignore it...

Have just given melatonin... please let it kick in soon - don't you just love 'em!!

11.20 pm

Still going strong, have managed to keep him in his room. Can now hear high-pitched squeaking to the tune of "London bridge is falling down."

12th March 2012
Spitting... again

G has been spitting and laughing almost continuously. He knows he's not meant to do it – I see his lips pursing, stare him out until he stops and looks away for a bit, then he looks back at me and does it anyway, laughing.

It is difficult not to see this as goading behaviour, he is really pushing my buttons now.

During the course of the evening he has also found some body lotion, a little spray to clean the computer screen, a small bottle of essential oil and a bottle of menthol. All are ominously empty.

After gobbing on the floor behind Annie's back as she is doing something (I can see him over her shoulder) I march him upstairs for the umpteenth time, this time lashing the dressing gown cord around the handle so he can't get out.

This sounds worse than it is... it's not a tight fit and there's a lot of slack so he could probably get out if he was persistent. All right, I know, I know, I'm not proud, and pretty damn far from perfect...

Later after Annie has gone home he is a lot quieter so I let him out. It's now 11.15pm.

I tell him slowly and clearly:

"You spit one more time and you're shut in your room again."

He comes downstairs. 5 minutes go by when I catch him spitting again.

Oh well. Not sure what time he'll go to sleep tonight.

Update: well it was probably about half past midnight that he finally went to sleep. I went in to turn his light off and found that he had managed to get out of his back-fastening sleepsuit, the nappy was off and there was poo stuck under his fingernails.

Thankfully it wasn't all over the bed clothes too.

16th March 2012
Language

In the car on the way home:
"Granddad's house... fire... smoke... cooking... toast... fork!"
Random.

21st March 2012
Stress!

4.30pm
I am talking on the phone to the OT giving her an update. Things aren't too bad at the moment but G is spitting, and H is getting OCD about certain things. Like my failure to repeat words back to him despite my being in another room where I can't hear him properly – silly Mummy! ("H going to school – yes!!") Or him going all "sock police" on G for wearing odd socks / one sock / no socks – delete as applicable. As the OT points out: these are little things that have a big impact, like me going quietly insane.

5pm
The estate agent has phoned to congratulate me on our house purchase. (Just so you know it wasn't a bungalow in the end, oh well.) Unfortunately H has recently had a little wobble: "Help G!!" (This is because of the sock police issue mentioned above – G had odd socks on.)
As a result of this wobble H has tried to hurt his hand and now wants me to kiss it better. I'm kissing his hand as quietly as I can in-between talking to the agent. This isn't good enough for H. He is getting increasingly louder waving his hand in my face: "Mummy kiss it better...mwah... MWAH!!!!"
I'm not really keen on blowing kisses apparently down the phone to the estate agent so H goes into full-on meltdown screaming mode.

At which point I terminate the call.

22nd March 2012
Random logic

H, after school on a sunny day: "Hot outside!"
He then blows the "outside" with his lips to cool it off.

Brushing past a parked car, he pulls me back to it and strokes the wing mirror: "Sorry."

Poking my belly button through my T shirt: "Sunshine!" (No idea on this one!)

Chapter 5

Patience is a virtue

I'm actually a pretty easy going girl. I had a happy childhood, and being laid back is probably the by-product of having 3 big brothers. For instance I had a poncho in the 70s (anyone remember those? Yes, I am that old). My brothers delighted in re-naming it the "punch-o" – gleefully pummelling me every time I wore it.

We also used to go and play hide and seek (or commandos as we called it, sounds much cooler!) up on the common. Years later I learned that when I was "it" my brothers actually just went off home and left me to it, only to be sent back to get me later by Mum.

So I am a pretty patient person. Just as well... God knows what I would have been like if I wasn't!

March 2012
Annie's story: Angry, angry G!

H had been upset and stressed out again earlier in the evening; I was going out, leaving Annie with the boys.
In Annie's words:

7.35pm:
Mum only left 15 minutes ago... H is still sniffling miserably on the sofa: don't think this is the last of his meltdown!

G however has been climbing on the desk, chucking stuff around, trying to hurt me. When unable to hurt me he heads for H. He then pushes at me and tugs at my clothes when I refuse to let him grab and hurt my hands. He then goes back upstairs, strips off and pulls his nappy apart – which is dirty I might add!

Ok, so I dunk him in the bath, just a quick one as I can still hear H muttering downstairs... then put G in a sleepsuit that he shouldn't be able to get out of and go back down.

I have to sort out more cuddles and drying of eyes for H. By the time we're done I find G has come down and is monkeying around on top of the cooker!

8.10pm

G is still climbing on everything and trying to hurt me. He has managed to dislodge the loft hatch and chuck it on the floor. He's either banging his head on the floor or trying to hurt H or me.

He has had 2 pairs of socks on already that have since been lost and I refuse to put any more on! Of course this makes him even angrier with me!!

8.30pm

H went to bed without any more fuss although to be honest I was expecting something...

9.15pm

G is still bouncing around and climbing everywhere. Hit me a few times.

Had his medicine around 9pm so it should start working soon, well I hope so anyway! He is like a naughty toddler crossed with a stroppy teenager! It's a strange mix and I'm unsure how to handle it.

9.25pm

G is quiet so I've just gone up to check, he's on his Mum's bed but not asleep yet. I'm not disturbing him, I don't care where he sleeps!

28th March 2012
The importance of release / one Mum's ramblings!

OK I got a bit serious writing this one, I even shed a tear or two as these things are hard for me to articulate — you have been warned!!

You get used to being the Mum of 2 kids with autism; it becomes your full-time job, your area of expertise. Same as most other parents, your kids are the love of your life, and you would do anything to protect them.
Maybe not quite the same is the calibre of the relentless, constant concerns centred around your children. Their behavior: the self-harming variety particularly hard to take, their future in our society, how well they will function, will they be able to support themselves, will they be ok?

I am incredibly lucky in finding supportive friends who "get it." I can't stress enough how different life would be if these people hadn't touched my life and offered to share in our crazy experiences. I'm pretty sure they have helped save my sanity along the way.

Finding something, an activity that momentarily removes these worries is also precious.
Singing with a bunch of friends does this for me. While I'm there I don't forget about my boys; no. But I forget about all the stuff mentioned above. One of the other ladies said that it made her forget about the physical pain that she was constantly in. I guess that's what music does for us.

Recently there has been a chance to audition for something that would be a fantastic experience, something that I'd never think I would have had the opportunity to do.
(Note: 1st June 2012: At the initial time of writing this we were all sworn to secrecy about it. This was actually a chance to sing on the official Diamond Jubilee record "Sing", plus an additional chance to be among those singing in London at the Jubilee concert in front of the Queen.)
Focussing on that, working towards that, blocked out everything. Not just for a couple of hours, it was doing a good job of keeping it all at bay for days on end: bonus!! Not to mention we are currently

buying a house and I wasn't even thinking about that!

When I didn't make it through the audition I was gutted, pure and simple. But I was truly happy for the singers that made it through, all lovely people with great voices. When that goal had been removed though I initially felt bereft, bitterly disappointed. But when I thought about it, it was the absence of those feelings that lurk in your mind all the time that I missed, as well as the missed singing opportunity.

Because there are other things that prey on our mind, that are consciously buried somewhere at the bottom as we find these ones more difficult to deal with. How will I cope with 2 severely autistic fully grown men... will I cope when I'm old, have to put my beautiful boys in care... and especially, what will happen to my dear ones after I am gone?

So... I am sure there will be other goals to work towards. In the meantime however, singing with people who also love to sing really is a fantastic release for me personally, and I am so grateful to have that opportunity.

I love to play the piano, but making music in a communal fashion; I had forgotten how satisfying and how much fun it could be. It's given me back a little of myself that has nothing to do with autism, and for that I am truly thankful.

29th March 2012
Tired times

9.40 pm

OK this may have been a bad idea as G is still going strong in his room and I've taken a sleeping tablet... I'll see you all on the other side!!!

30th March 2012
5am: eyes on!

Managed to convince H "No phone game, time for sleep!"
Lasted about half an hour before I got told: "Eyes on!!" Funny lad!

31st March 2012
Being in different places

So H had his first overnight stay at a residential respite unit last night. He didn't get out of bed in the night at all.
Hmm…

1st April 2012
H's Sunday night nightmare routine

10pm
H went to bed at approximately 8.40pm. Since then he has come out of bed 14 times, on seemingly tiny pretexts.
First, the green radio didn't have 3 lights on it: this actually only happens when the battery is failing, but try telling H that.

OK, 15 times now as I'm typing this.

Each time I have to say "Night night, sleep tight. Stay in bed like a good boy, good boy for staying in bed." Sometimes I don't say it correctly, H will then prompt me to say it again, getting quite distressed if it's not done the right way.
Unfortunately after the 5th time my repetition of the phrases has got more and more curt, interspersed with "Get to bed NOW!" This isn't pleasing to H either. And I know: yelling at an autistic child who is already in a state of high alert is not a good plan.

Several times we have had "H crying, don't cry H, wipe your eyes, Mummy cuddle, Mummy sleep…" etc. Oh yes, I've also had to "move" the toy, duvet, and cat rug that he likes put over his arms each time as well. This endless round of repetition is making me feel rather certifiable I'm afraid.
The latest attempt to get me to go to my bed and have him in it too, started with him asking for the white radio that is by my bed. Very crafty. Had to turn the radio on for one second to pre-empt yet another meltdown, then off again. He now has the white radio in his room. Hopefully this will work as I am getting decidedly ratty. I am a patient person but I'm afraid I am now taking time out to yell

muffled obscenities into my pillow.

10.15pm
Damn, now he wants a drink. 16 times.

10.17pm
17 times. He has now come downstairs saying "H upset, Mummy upstairs."
Now he has stripped his PJs and asked for a new nappy.
Please, please, PLEASE... let this be the last time.

10.22pm
He is back in bed. Half an hour ago I was contemplating the merits of a soundproof rubber room with a punch bag in it that I could shut myself in. Now I'm just emotionally and physically drained.

10.30pm
Fingers crossed it has gone quiet. Now I just need to get G to bed. Did I mention he was still up?

8th April 2012
Playground antics

H is on the helter-skelter slide, and comes down too fast before the other child is off, clonking him in the back with his feet.
Thankfully the little lad is fine, just looks a bit confused.
H goes through his ritual of "Little boy hurt, cuddle little boy, little boy sticker..." etc. H doesn't seem too stressed though as the little lad didn't actually cry.
We move away from the slide and sit on a bench. H has finished the usual ritual of words, now he is randomly coming out with other phrases: "Little boy water... little boy snowman... little boy haircut... hurt haircut..."
OK cutting hair - hurt... maybe?! But snowman??!

17th April 2012
"Move..."

Had to stop the car on the way home today so I could answer a phone call. Was on the phone for a few minutes when H started asking me to "Move bag."
It was on the floor of the rear footwell as we have had issues with the bag before. There was a time the flap wasn't closed properly and was caught on the edge of the seat. This time however I'm not sure what the problem is - OCD?!

I spend the next 10 minutes with an increasingly distraught H playing tug of war with the bag, me trying to shift the bag minute degrees, while H just holds it in place, whilst still yelling "Move!!"
I somehow manage to pacify him and we get home. H is sitting on the stairs to take his shoes off. The shoes are not sitting just so and H is telling me to "move" the shoes. I try to put them together at the side of the stairs where they usually go. That's no good, today they have to be in the middle of the step.
Next he is sitting on the sofa with the phone game. Finally he gets his knickers in a twist over the blanket.
"Move up..." We pull the blanket up to cover the back of the sofa. No, no good. We end up compromising by pulling the top bit over the seat back and having the rest over the seat.

"Move" has now become a word which strikes terror into my heart...

17th April 2012
"Sticker telly..."

Following on from the twitchiness earlier...
The boys have been in the garden with Annie. Things have been a little twitchy as H has found a new "game" of tackling G to the floor on the trampoline mid-bounce.
They come inside. H has his ipod when he notices G has picked up a shoe: he still wants to go out! H tries to snatch the shoe away, a tug of war ensues. G pats H's head to tell him to get away, H whacks G, I pull them apart.

I'm dealing with G in the hall when the next thing I know I hear H yelling, and Annie tells me he has lobbed the ipod at the telly.

Yep, it's knackered.

The LCD-ness of it is bleeding across the screen.

I march H upstairs – "You do NOT throw things!" I'm afraid there might have been a couple of rude words here. I shut him in his room, where he yells for "disk!" I tell him no and prudently remove the potential weapons of the DVD player and the radio.

There's a lot of screaming, thrashing about etc, then eventually we go through the "pick up... cuddle..." phase.

Downstairs he goes and pinches Annie on the chest.

I march him out and sit him on the stairs. More screaming. I cup my hand to my ear and say "listen" a few times, then when he pauses for breath I launch in with "You do not hurt Marianne!! Say sorry to Marianne!"

He gives Annie a cuddle.

Then we have to put a "sticker" on the telly and take it off again and clean the telly with a tissue. Funnily enough to H's distress this does not fix the telly.

Eventually things calm down but it's all hellish twitchy. H spends the rest of the evening watching disks on the DVD player and doesn't touch the phone game.

The next day I am still getting "Marianne sticker!"

Then, on the way home from school:

"Hammer television... (flap hands) fix television... (flap hands) Mummy hammer... (flap hands) television sad... (flap hands) clean television..." well you get the picture...

When we get home I have to mime "hammering" the telly, then clean it with a tissue. After this I say "Telly still broken."

I have to do this on and off over the next 3 days, each time saying "Telly still broken" which H repeats.

I have borrowed a portable TV which I hide during the day and trundle out at night when H is in bed as I want him to know that "broken" in this case lasts more than just a moment.

19th April 2012
Multiple baths: good thing we're not on a water meter

Annie met us at the Thrift Shop today for our usual visit. H sits down next to my friend's boy with his ipod plugged in. The shop is quite busy with a lot of helpers in so we are yacking and laughing amongst ourselves. Foolishly I have forgotten my 2 boys with sensory issues... oops.

H: "We're going home."
We manage to fob him off by sitting him round the back in the changing room where it's quiet. This works for a bit but then he starts getting twitchy again. OK we are nearly ready to go so start getting things together.
H picks up a tagging gun, fixating on trying to pull off the end plastic tags. Sadly they are too strong and despite me saying "Mummy help" we have a bit of a tug of war with the tag gun. (I do win this one you'll be pleased to know.) We are on opposite sides of the counter when G appears on H's side.
Uh oh... I just know this isn't going to go well...

I barrel around the counter yelling "excuse me!" but it's too late, the boys have locked on to each other, H having a handful of G's hair. I manage to pull them apart but all hell breaks loose.
H whacks down on the floor and is screaming his lungs out on one side of me, G is grinding his chin into my arm and hand on the other. We eventually get out and back to the car safely, then off home.
I tell H he is having a bath. Annie takes him up no problem, but he then insists on running the cold tap and wants to come out before being washed, yanking the plug out. Oh well never mind.
Downstairs, pj's on.
"Bath!" Hmm, ok back up. Pj's off again.
"Plug off, plug on, cold water on..." A bit more faffing and I manage to get him washed this time. I say bath finished then we go down, pj's on.
"H bath!"
Oh dear.
"H shower, shower bath, shower head..." For goodness sake he doesn't even like his hair washed let alone with a shower!

Annie takes him up as he's really getting quite stressed about the shower. She runs the shower for a few seconds into the bath as we really don't want to undress him yet again. He's not really too happy with this but we manage to move him on to his supper. He is actually asking for bed now.

We hustle him through the bedtime routine: bedtime can't come quick enough.

21st April 2012
Should've known better!

So we've bought a house that needs some work doing before we move in. We foolishly believed that it would be ok for Steve to go and do a few jobs with just G for company. Kind of forgot about G's obsession with spraying water. Hindsight is a wonderful thing.

Two flooded bathrooms and a wrecked ceiling later...

21st April 2012
Annie's Story: "Moving" things again

In Annie's words:

Well this is fun!

For the last 45 minutes H has been in meltdown mode - just what I need when G is wanting to go out! H got twitchy about where the cable for the ipod charger was laying. This soon moved from twitchy to complete meltdown as neither him nor I can settle the cable to where it makes him happy.

Oh great! Now not only am I supposed to mind-read, I'm also supposed to guess something that he doesn't even seem to know!

So he throws the ipod. Tantrum now in full swing... he's pulling at the plug so hard I think the whole thing might come out of the wall, so I take the plug away and say it's gone... tantrum now doubled!! My thinking is he will get over this, I hope so...

Ok so an hour later he asks for his room and disk upstairs. I agree and take him upstairs with the disk and ipod. I'm praying these don't get thrown across the room but am thinking he needs to chill out!

So for the next 15 minutes he stays upstairs quietly while I reassure G that the world is not ending! I go up to H and say nappy change, pyjamas then yogurt... I repeat what the bedtime routine will be and he comes downstairs. I get him changed and sat at the table with disk and yogurt... for an extra 5 minutes chill out he sits on the sofa with disk, before book, teeth and BED... hopefully!!
Ok, well at 9.30pm H is asleep after repeating his bedtime routine twice!
G was asleep by 8.45pm: he went and hid from H in his room and fell asleep without melatonin!

G must've been stressed to give in to sleep so easily!

22nd April 2012
Playing together nicely - it does happen!

A lovely sight to see earlier:
H tickling G's neck while both boys were giggling - and there was no whacking, hair pulling or eye gouging anywhere!

These little things are huge steps in a household like ours.
Right now this moment is very welcome as a tiny oasis in an increasingly stressful period...

Chapter 6

Crisis approaching, batten down the hatches

The whole time from after Easter things have been getting steadily more difficult: I'm finding it hard to keep smiling sometimes, though of course the smile is usually a slightly demented one!!

24th April 2012
Sleeping tablet, 2am visit from G and H trying to drag me out of bed by the thumbs, equals grumpy Mummy plus stressed H!!

9.45 pm
I take a sleeping tablet.

2am
Crap. G is up and waving food packets in my face. A little difficult to wake up at this point but I manage a semi-comatose state.

2.35am
I get G a drink and a small bunch of Pringles crisps and stick him back in his room, lashing the door shut with a dressing gown cord.

I really don't advocate imprisoning my children but no dressing gown cord equals stumbling around the house for the next 4 hours minimum, trying to keep an eye on him whilst trying not to look at the inside of my eyelids.

Dressing gown cord on equals a bit of squeaking from G's room where he is safe, and the possibility of sleeping again that night.

6.50am

H is trying to pull me out of bed by the thumbs. I'm afraid in my sleeping tablet induced hangover I'm rather grumpy at the prospect and refuse.

"Mummy get up!!"

"No! Get off!"

Interval of yelling on H's part and grumbling on mine.

"H go downstairs, Mummy's having a rest."

"Mummy sleep, cuddle, sticker head (after he's slapped it), disk."

"Disk H's room."

We go to his room.

"H lie down, have a rest." I put his DVD on.

H pointing: "See the moon."

Me: "Ok yes see the moon."

"Moon!!" Agitated. "See that there, moon!"

There is no moon as it's daylight through the curtains now. I do my best to pull the curtains closer to block the light out.

"Moon... moon... that there... help..."

I'm getting as stressed as he is now!

Me: "Show Mummy where to help."

"You want that there, see that there..."

I have a bit of a brainwave and take an educated guess - I think it's that the curtain on one side is less opaque than the other.

Me opening curtains: "Moon finished, daylight outside."

This seems to sort things a little. We then go through the whole cuddle routine, stay in bed like a good boy etc.

A couple of minutes after this the alarm goes off anyway. Right, time to get up. God, I feel like I'm walking through treacle. I guess sleeping pills work better when you've not had interrupted sleep.

Off we go downstairs. I really need to sort G out for when his bus comes. H has other ideas and starts having mini OCD moments about the blanket not lying correctly. He has his ipod but starts asking for the "white radio" which lives in our bedroom.

Me: "White radio is in Mummy's room!"

H: "White radio Mummy upstairs yes!!"

I'm getting quite stressed now cos I really need to do G's nappy, dress him and prepare his medicine.

I finally compromise by bringing the white radio downstairs. I didn't want to, but the other option was to be immersed in one of H's full-flow meltdowns when I just didn't have the time.

25th April 2012
Night-time OCD!

3am
H gets up with a dirty nappy – unfortunately the last couple of days he has moved from his usual pooing time of 5pm-ish.

4am
H comes in complaining about the blanket / cat rug that he has laid across his bed. I manage to stumble up and sort this out without too much hassle. Put his disk back on and I go back to bed.

5am
Oh boy, pretty tired now. I'm not sure if H has even gone back to sleep in-between times. Sadly this time he is more insistent in the correct rug-laying procedure. I spend the next 5 minutes trying to sort the rug...

"Move cat rug... move that there..."

After attempting to re-arrange the rug H starts saying he wants the big toy dog's "feet under". Then another battle and tug of war ensues with the dog, duvet and the cat rug. At one point I am getting "Eyes under" too.

I try resolving the issue by saying "dog fine... cat rug ok..." etc but it's not really happening.

Oh dear we are fixating back on the cat rug again, he starts pushing it down the bed, saying "Move that there!"

Me, removing the rug: "Cat rug off?"
H: "Cat rug on!!"
Rats, that wasn't it.

After about 10 minutes of increasing agitation from H, and an increasing amount of goose bumps on me (it's quite chilly with no dressing gown on... I did get up in rather a hurry) I squeeze into bed alongside him pulling the duvet over us both.
H: "Mummy's bed."
For once I am happy to oblige.
Into my bed we get.
"Radio on."

On it goes on the lowest volume.
In goes my ear plug.

25th April 2012
H learning to help himself

It's been raining quite heavily on the way home from school, and there are raindrops on the inside of the car door and his car seat.
"Clean, Mummy help!"
Me: "H can clean, H is a big boy!!" My voice was incredibly over the top in the encouragement stakes here.
"Tissue!"
I give him a tissue and he wipes the seat and door clean.

Again, little steps!

26th April 2012
Night-time OCD: it's become a habit...

2.20am
Fretting about the cat rug again. 5 minutes of re-settling, disk back on...
Proceeds to sing and chat along to the "Night Garden" for the next

hour VERY loudly.

3.30am
"Big Pooh... help Big Pooh...!!"
Oh God. He's totally stressing about Big Pooh: he hasn't even got him in his bed, he has Big Dog instead. I try to remove Big Dog and swap him for Pooh.
No. Not happening. Quite a bit of stress later I manage to escape whilst saying "Stay in bed like a good boy, good boy for staying in bed..."
5 minutes later he is in my bed. Oh well.

5am
G is singing very loudly in his room – what is with the loud singing tonight?!

5.30am
It's time to get up with G then, as he has blasted into my bedroom at full squeak mode. Luckily H is so knackered he sleeps through it.

26th April 2012
Annie's story - Severe meltdown

This next bit was related to me by Annie as I was out for the evening.

H has been really "twitchy" all this week. Annie's not sure what the trigger was this time but when he had a nappy change he asked for "disk – nappy". The disk was still playing and he could hear it but he couldn't see the screen. When the telly was working though, it's not like he could see the telly when having a new nappy either.
Not sure of the details after this, but H went into FULL meltdown.

He was trying to hit Annie, but mostly he was trying to hurt himself; badly. Screaming and grabbing things to whack himself on the head.
Usually we let him scream and cry it out on the floor but Annie had serious concerns about H hurting himself so understandably couldn't stand by and watch this. H seems to have no limits to his behaviour if a meltdown can't be resolved.

Annie pulled H on her lap facing away from her and wrapped her arms around his, restraining him. He was trying to fight her with arms and legs all the way. After about 5 minutes she felt his whole body relax, then he asked for a cuddle etc.

That night he was still very difficult to get to bed: whatever position Big Pooh was in H must be in exactly the same position.

Eventually around 9.45pm H went into my bed and said "Green radio Mummy's room". Once left in my bed he only prompted Annie to repeat one phrase: "Stay in bed like a good boy." Then he settled down.

Toeing up to the line... step away... step right back... that's it...

There was a time, some years ago now, that things were really tough. It had always been difficult, but I suppose it was the first time that things had intensified to such a level, out of the norm.

G was screaming an awful lot then: not just loud, but so high-pitched it actually made my ears rush, like when you hear a smoke alarm, or burglar alarm. He was around 5 or 6 years old.

He would furiously bang his head while doing this. If I was witnessing the headbutting it just seemed to make him worse. I tried various things. If I put him in the garden to try to stall this behaviour he would headbutt the brick wall of the house. He permanently had a bald patch in the middle of his hairline where he scraped his head along the carpet.

I tried putting him in his room to give him some time out. Putting him in his room was actually not easy either, I would plonk him on his mattress. The bed frame and other furniture had been removed as advised by the professionals involved. They thought there was too much stimulus in his room, which was impeding his sleep routine.

As soon as I put him down he would fly full pelt at the door, almost before I had closed it. He was coming at me so fast, the "plonking down" soon became a shove back into the room, until I was almost throwing him away from me so I could slam the door in time. We then repeated this behaviour on a loop, the whole thing punctuated by violent headbanging.

I knew the lady from the terrace 2 doors up. She told me later she could feel and hear the reverberations of G's head hitting the floorboards in her house.

After an hour or so of this, the shoving became more and more pronounced. I was actually picking him up and throwing him on to the mattress to give myself time to slam the door before he could wedge his fingers around the door frame. It was then that I was actually visualising throwing him across his bedroom, against the wall, anywhere, away from me – anything to get him to stop. Worse, for a split second I wanted to backhand him, I was almost shaking inside with the desire to do it – though desire is totally the wrong word, as whoever wants to do that?? But before you call social services on me: I never hurt my boy.

But I know what it's like to be desperate; desperate to stop the incessant screaming, stop him flying at me with hooked gouging fingers. But mostly to stop the self-harming, that absolutely breaks your heart to see. I have toed up to the line that shouldn't be crossed and glimpsed through the doorway. I didn't like what I was imagining in my mind's eye so I stepped away. I immediately took myself out of the equation. Instead of trying to keep him safe in his room, I simply took myself into mine. I sat down against the door, blocking it shut, and sobbed; while my dear boy hurled himself repeatedly at the other side.

I am so lucky now in that I have friends to turn to. Then it was different. I had friends, but I didn't feel at the time that they were the sort of friends that I could go and have a cuppa with, and talk about the fact that I had been very close to hurting my child, my dear lad. Unthinkable. Not the sort of thing you launch into with just anyone.
At that time I had help from a lady with the boys for 8 hours a month. It was her I reached out to, asking if she was in. I think she heard the desperation in my voice, and immediately asked me round for a brew, so I left G with Steve and took little H with me.

It was a turning point for me, as it's a hard thing to do; to ask for help.
I was actually told by one speech therapist that I smiled and laughed too much, it looked like I was coping. Really?! When you're laughing about how great it is that you're shattered all the time, don't they hear the sarcasm, the edge of hysteria? I guess not.

After this experience, I know that there is a line I'll never cross; because I recognise the onset of extreme emotions that can bring you to this point. I was a pretty placid person to start with, but I have learnt patience on a grand scale.
Oh you'll see that I've been desperate again, and there have been times when I've

been close to visualising those actions again. And I know I've smacked their bums. Both of them. But it's been a very rare thing, and I hope I'll never do that again, as I remember the resentment I felt when smacked as a child.

And I have moved on from those initial desperate times: I hope I understand my boys better now, and that we are all happier as a result.

It's a pretty hard thing to write because it is a taboo subject. But if you're going to write about the stresses of day to day living with the clash between autistic and neurotypical mind, heightened by sleep deprivation, then there's no point in not being honest about it. Especially when there are very challenging behaviours involved.

This is why respite and practical support is so, so important for people like us, all of us: parents and children.

27th April 2012
BLACK Friday

A truly awful, awful morning. Have been crying for about an hour and a half now as I start writing this!

H had slept fairly well in my bed with me. Got up around 7.45am, seemed quite happy. I let him play the 2 Facebook games that he had been stressing about yesterday, so that was fine. First game had finished (no lives left, H understands this) and was playing the second with a bit of breakfast by his side.

Then: "Wet trousers, trousers off." Ok the nappy had leaked a little. He wasn't stressing, so I changed his nappy. H then decided he wanted wet trousers back on.

Me: "Wet trousers off, dry school trousers on."

Spent the next 10 minutes having a fight where H wouldn't release the wet pj's. He forced both his legs into one of the pyjama legs and managed to stand up. I hoped this would get it out of his system so we could move on.

Then: "Nappy off..." He's just had a new nappy...!

"Nappy off... pants on!"

Oh ok, he wants the pull-ups on that he has at school. I tear off the nappy I've just put on 10 minutes ago.

"Nappy on!!" Oh crap.

He now won't let me put the pull-up on but wants his nappy back on. The same one I've just ripped off. Unfortunately these nappies aren't good at being re-sealed. A screaming bout ensues while I physically struggle with the nappy.

Somewhere around this point I start crying and am unable to stop. I'm just so tired of this. In the throes of his meltdown H doesn't *seem* to notice this at all, but I'm sure that's not true.

In the end I agree to put the original nappy back on. Thankfully I managed to rip the outer tab away and use the still sticky under-tab. We're all good.
I manage to get the school trousers on plus the rest of his clothes. Am just about to put his shoes on when he says "Trousers off!!" and strips them off – I just can't keep them on him. He then wants nappy off, and says he wants pants again.
Me: "School, then pants on." (When changed at school he has the pull-ups put on so this isn't a fib!)
Some more agro, then I scribble on a piece of paper: "Trousers on, then shoes on, then car, then school" and point it out to him while I read it.
I am really losing the plot now and am about to get him in the car as he is and chuck his clothes in a bag. Suddenly H wants the school trousers on.

Ok shoes on, lock door. We are going to the car when H starts screaming for the bubble pop game again. He is yelling "Home" as well. The next bit I think we were both screaming at each other: I'm not proud, I'm simply human.

I'm trying to drag him to the car; he's resisting. (Resisting is actually quite a mild term for it!) In the end I somehow manage to pick him up by threading one arm between his legs and the other under his arm. We get a few steps before I have to put this flailing bundle down. I'm grabbing his arm saying "stand up" and "walk". We get to the car where he won't let me push him into the car, no way. After a few more minutes of me repeating "H's chair!" he yells "Cuddle!!"
Me: "H's chair, then cuddle."
I get him in, manage to shut the door despite him pushing at it, he is

yelling some more.

We drive to school with him screaming and both of us crying.

He gets out of the car at school, drops down on his knees which I then have to rub better, then quite happily walks in with me.

We get to the classroom door when H says "Pants on, school" and wants to cuddle me. I'm still crying through this so another TA takes H to assembly while I explain to his one-to-one what's happened. 20 minutes later the class comes back. I'm still crying - for goodness sake, I can't stop! H is all smiles and walks past me to his desk without a second glance.

I really don't know what's going on the last few days, I'm about to phone the occupational therapist (OT). They are supposed to help with situations to stop them from getting to crisis point, but this behaviour has escalated so fast I feel we are already there!

I'd mentioned to the OT about his night-time OCD on Wednesday, yesterday I saw the paediatrician for G but mentioned H there too. She is going to write to the Psychologist. But the situation has doubled in intensity overnight!!

Afternoon

Phoned the OT who subsequently spoke to the social worker about emergency respite. After spending the last few hours crying (or trying not to cry!) and having a little go on the piano, the social worker suggested it would be better to have a helper with me to pick up H and then be at home with me. She was concerned as I'd said I couldn't bear the thought of picking him up from school only to be right back where we left off.

Appended in December 2012: What was actually going through my mind, over and over again, were the words "I can't...I can't..."
I wouldn't even let myself finish the unthinkable thought, as what I was trying not to think, was that I couldn't go on; I couldn't see how I could do this much longer. I didn't feel I was doing a very good job of parenting at all and I did wonder if he would be better off without me. Even to write that on the day it happened was not acceptable to me.

Going to school for H is a bit like going to Narnia then coming back through the wardrobe: school time is generally all happy and ok, but the moment I pick him up at the end of the day he is back to remembering what happened in the morning. We have gone back to that moment as if nothing has gone between.

The social worker also said I should see if Steve could get home earlier from his work away: thank God it's Friday and he will be back later! Annie was free after tea but not before, so a friend, bless her, after listening to me prattle on about it all in the Thrift Shop where I help out, arranged it so she could come to school with me to get H. I felt a bit better after this, wasn't dreading the pick-up so much.

So we got H. As he came down the stairs at school he wasn't his usual smiling self, he had a very dead-pan look on his face. Didn't get my usual pick-up squeezy hug greeting, and he just parroted back whatever we said to him. Was fine though: got home, my friend read to him and played with cars etc. Then when G was back she went on the trampoline with him, H followed for a bit.

Everything was ok for a while. Steve got back from his week at work just before Annie got here, so Steve and I went out for a curry so we could chat. I really needed to talk to him.

Annie's story: bad evening

In Annie's words:

H is all smiles but after this week I'm feeling a little weary! So anyway he seems ok. I toast him a hot cross bun and he sits and eats, all happy and smiles... ok this H I can handle!!

I run H a bath and put a little "relaxing bath soak" in it. We can but hope! I get H ready and before we even get up the stairs he is muttering: "Bath is...? Blue tap... blue tap feet..." He's getting a little twitchy. I just agree and go with the ritual, get him in the bath. Let's hope he comes out still smiley...!

"Clean bubbles!!!" Suddenly he doesn't want bubbles in the bath and starts to scream! Yes clean bubbles, H clean... note to self, DO NOT put bubbles in H's bath!!

"Bubbles nose... bubbles mouth... Marianne get clean..."

I just do as he asks like a puppet!

We get downstairs and put nappy and pj's on.

"Marianne sad, oh no..."

"Marianne's not sad, H that's funny!"

"Marianne glasses off, H glasses on, Marianne sad... YES!!"

"Marianne not sad, Marianne happy... see – smiles! H is funny!"

He does his funny forced laugh. Please let that be the end of it... don't want a meltdown tonight!!!

Ok time for bedtime routine... he's twitchy about yogurt and disk but ok, we got through that... Book: again twitchy but kind of more fidgety than twitchy.

Clean teeth, fine. Sit on toilet, did a poo! Lots of praise!!

Got into bed, I tucked him up as usual, made sure the duvet was at the same level for him as it was for Pooh bear, switched on DVD... said goodnight and only went through the verbal ritual ONCE!! Can now hear him reciting the book out loud. Hope he stays up there!!

Oh my God spoke too soon...

Well that was Annie's bit, we got a couple of frantic text messages so left the Indian restaurant early. Takeaway cartons are a wonderful thing.
Here's the gist of what happened next.

Annie had mistakenly put some new pj's on H not realising until too late that the top had short sleeves...

"Sleeves down!!"

Naturally she wasn't allowed to take the existing short-sleeve top off to replace it with a long-sleeved one.

Cue meltdown.

He ended up throwing the DVD player against the wall, then threw it at Annie's head. That girl doesn't get paid anywhere near enough.

He was in bed when we got back but still awake and agitated.

Managed to settle him down after this.

28th April 2012
McDonald's meltdown

Repeat performance of Friday morning's behaviour, this time we had been in McDonald's, and quite happily had lunch. We were sitting in one of the booths with immoveable bench seats: note the word "immoveable" here. After the meal H was laying back along the seat pushing his feet against the wall.

Then came the dreaded words...

"Move chair..."

Eeek!!

What followed was pretty hideous. Manhandling a kicking and screaming H out of a quite crowded McDonald's, I sent Steve ahead to the car with the bags.

I got as far as the middle of the drive-through road when I just got stuck with him and had to yell to Steve for help. I was trying to get H back to the car and out of the roadway. I had a kind of hold of him, sort of half managed to pick him up. Unfortunately this meant my hands were occupied and I couldn't stop him from pinching and gouging my neck, and ripping at my lip making it bleed.

Steve came over and manhandled him into the car with a few (not very nice!!) words. I've not seen him look so angry in a long time, and he's a pretty easy going guy.

After managing to wedge him in his seat H was still going for it – I lay across his body trying to pin him down and put his seatbelt on. After a few minutes he calmed enough so that we could drive home safely.

Steve and I were pretty much silent for this journey.

28th April 2012
Bedtime with Annie

H goes to bed ok, though still in a twitchy mood. He is putting Annie through the usual verbal ritual of prompting her to say certain phrases.

Annie: "Night, night, sleep tight."

H then prompts her to say "Stay in bed like a good boy."

Then he says "Bye bye Marianne" and waves goodbye!!

This is a first for him, but she goes along with this and says "Goodbye H, night night."

30th April 2012
Bad bedtimes

H came out of his bedroom about 5 times. After I had been feeling increasingly annoyed and telling him to get back in his bed I heard him throw the DVD player on the floor. Yes, the new one. I went in there and smacked his padded bum. You can imagine how that went down. And no, I didn't feel good about myself.

Long story short: lots of repeatedly tucking him back in bed, ended up with Bedcat instead of Pooh, lots of death-grip hugs around the neck, me telling him "Mummy not sad, Mummy's angry because H won't stay in bed." And yes, I know, trying emotional blackmail now. You don't need to tell me this is not good.
I was seething inside, I'm afraid my patience for this sort of thing seems to be running thin.
I'm just so tired all the time...

1st May 2012
"Like a puppet on a string... la la la laaa"

H's ritualising of everything is getting really wearing; for example H wanting the phone game in bed with me upstairs. I tell him to get it. He doesn't. Then I say I must go downstairs as Julie (the bus escort) is coming. I have to say "see Julie then lie down upstairs" to stop H freaking out. After G has gone we are back to lying down upstairs. Curtains closed, shut the door, radio on, neck covered (his), phone game on. After a moment I am safe to get up and go downstairs again, but if I don't do all this first even for a moment there will be a meltdown. It's no wonder we're always late for school...

I feel like a puppet on a string, dancing to his insane tune of obsessive rituals...

2nd May 2012
Anxiety, OCD, or just "What did your last slave die of?"

Once awake in bed with me in the morning, H likes to go get his phone game and bring it into bed with me for a few minutes. He asks me to do it but on prompting gets it himself.
Now, however...

"Phone game pod, Mummy downstairs..."
Me: "H get phone game pod please, H is a big boy."
We have a few minutes of arguing the toss, then him hanging around on the landing whimpering. Eventually he goes downstairs after repeated prompting from me.
Then I hear sounds of distress: "Help!!" so I go down to investigate.
H has taken the phone game off the charger lead, but is now trying to minutely place the charger plug in a certain position. I don't precisely know what that position is, it's not stretched out straight or anything like that, it just obviously isn't right for H. A couple of minutes of high anxiety and we manage to resolve it and we go upstairs, lie down, radio on etc.

A few minutes later (time is of the essence here; G's bus is due and he's not dressed yet!!) I tell H Mummy is going downstairs.
I go.
H stands at the top of the stairs saying "Pick up downstairs."
He wants me to carry him down. Grrr.
We reach a compromise by me beckoning him down and pointing to the 3rd step: "Mummy pick up here."
H comes to the 4th step, pulls my hand up saying "pick up upstairs."
To forestall the brewing explosion I move up to stand on the bottom step, then pick him up and lift him down.
All is now ok.

3rd May 2012
Phone game on (death by transferred echolalia)

What follows is a fairly typical conversation: but this is especially bad in the mornings or evenings. If I don't repeat the phrases or noises as required by H he will ultimately go into meltdown, something I want to avoid.

The professionals involved tell me this is controlling behaviour, which isn't desirable from a 7 year old. Sod desirable, I think this boy's got me beat...

H: "Phone game on."
Me: "H get phone game on please."
H: "Phone game on?"
Me: "H do it."
H: "Phone game on!"
Me: "Yes, phone game on! H do it, H is a big boy!"
H: "Phone game on H do it." (Still looking expectantly at me.)
Me: "Yes, that's right."
H: "Phone game on, H do it!!!"
Me: "Phone-game-on-H-do-it-that's-right!!" (Breathe, breathe...)

2 minutes later...
H: "Phone game on."
Me: "H do it."
H: "H do it."
Pause... he's waiting for me to repeat, I know it...
H: "H do it."
Me: "Yes, H do it! Please H, Mummy doesn't want to keep saying it!!!"
2 minutes later...
H: "Phone game on."
Me: "Yes, phone game on! H do it, H is a big boy!"
H: "Phone game on H do it."
Me: "Yes, that's right."
H: "Phone game on!!"

Breathe...

Me: "PHONE GAME ON PHONE GAME ON PHONE GAME ON PHONE GAME ON PHONE GAME OOONNN!!!!!!!" (Happy thoughts, happy thoughts...)
H: "Huu-uhh?" (Little bit difficult to spell this questioning, irritated

sound!)

Me: silence.

H: "Huu-uhh?!!"

Here's the fun part, I have to repeat the noise he makes precisely. I oblige, through gritted teeth, in a rather forceful manner.

Silence.

H: "Phone game on."

Me: "Phone game on! H do it!"

H: "H do it, H is a big boy!"

Oh boy.

4th May 2012
Bedtime book – it's a little late (or early?!)

(A quick note: last year the doctor suggested giving H some of G's melatonin to try to see if it would keep him asleep. Sadly I don't have a written record of this so have since been advised NOT to do this as I could get in trouble! Get it in writing folks!!)

Got H to bed last night after giving him 4ml melatonin at 8.20pm. Have been doing this for a few days now. Only had to do bedtime ritual once before he fell asleep: marvellous!

Unfortunately H woke at 1am. He's been doing this since he started the melatonin too, nothing unusual in that except he's not going straight back to sleep. This has been happening a bit even before the meds though, so there's probably no significance in that.

So anyway, at 1am he demands his bedtime book again, clean teeth, sit on toilet, the works.

Back to bed.

Wakes up again about 6am, starts asking for the book again. I manage to fob him off a bit but in the meantime he has me putting him back in his bed with the radio from my room (which stops working – great!), the disk, then his green radio. Then he's back in with me again.

Eventually after repeated badgering we go downstairs to do the book at 7.30am. I figure I better do it now as I really need to get G up for school soon.

So we do the book, clean teeth, get into bed, big Pooh in bed, radio on, cat rug over arms etc (no toilet this time): that's got to be a record for the latest – or earliest - bedtime routine yet!!

7th May 2012
Cuddles with G

I have a VERY cuddly G lately... proper arms round neck, nose to nose, cheek to cheek cuddles... so lovely to have, I don't think I'll ever take that for granted!

9th May 2012
"Suffer the little children..."

Due to H being quite difficult lately, I decide that when I go to practice the piano in the church as part of my own respite, Annie and the boys can come with me, rather than leaving her to struggle alone.

There is a door out to a corridor, through another door to different rooms at the end.

Cue lots of excited cackling from the boys as G hares off down the corridor, Annie hot on his heels, and H gleefully bringing up the rear. Oh well they are happy.

Oops. Didn't realise the local scout group were practising for a parade in the end room. G gives Annie the slip twice to dart in there and run over the chairs. He's not keen on coming out and the scouts don't look amused. Eek!

There's a lot more sprinting up and down the corridor and around the church where I'm playing, interspersed with periods of H "duetting" with me. Poor Annie has stripped down to her vest top as it is incredibly hot in the church complex.

Next thing we know G is hoying on the bell rope and has put out an impromptu call to church... runaway amateur bellringer at work!!

10th May 2012
Managing mornings

Latest attempt to forestall morning meltdowns...

1.30am
H comes in to my room bearing the DVD player. "Disk off!" The power switch seems too stiff for him to work. I oblige and put it down on the floor. (I know I'm going to need this later!)
"Radio on." Radio goes on as low in volume as I can get it.
I attempt to go back to sleep.

You'll notice I have caved by letting him stay in my bed: I'm running on fumes most of the time and above all else I need to be able to continue to function in the day...

6.30am
"Disk Mummy's room." I put the DVD player on. See, I told you I would need it!

7.30am
"Mummy downstairs, disk downstairs." Ok. I get up.
"Mummy get H get downstairs." I have managed to cut this down to picking him up off the bed, then putting him down while I say: "Wheee... clonk!" He will then go downstairs by himself, as opposed to having a stress attack because I won't carry him down the stairs.
Thankfully G is still asleep.
I settle H down in the lounge with his phone game and a bowl of cereal bar and fruit. I then whip out to the hallway, turn the computer on, and surreptitiously lose 4 lives apiece from the 2 Facebook games he just *has* to play. They normally have 5 lives each, which could last some time!

7.45am
Get the key from the cabinet, unlock the front door and take the chain off so the bus escort can come straight in. Cutting it fine here but then whizz up the stairs (as fast as I can 'whizz' with my dodgy knee) to change and dress G who is still sparked out on his bed. I've

got his nappy done and trousers on when I hear the dreaded whining in the distance from H.

"H, what's the matter, come and tell Mummy please!"
The mumbling whine comes a bit closer into the hall downstairs: "Mummy shut the door!!"
Eh?
I hobble downstairs as fast as I can. "H show Mummy which door?"
Points: "That there."
I've left the door to the key cabinet open.

Whoops.

10th May 2012
Another day another meltdown...

We are driving home from school. We get as far as the last village before home when I hear... "Move plug on..."
He is very fidgety, and escalating fast so I stop the car to "help the plug on" as the charger lead for the phone game doesn't seem to be in the desirable place. Five minutes later after pulling, pushing, trying to put it in a slot between the seats etc I manage to get in the car and drive off again.

Unfortunately...

The drink bottle tips over in the holder, it has orange squash in it.
"Help orange drink!!"
Me: "Orange drink fine."
Then:
"Mummy get red drink!!"
"Home then red drink. We don't have any red drink in the car."
"Red drink car yes! Red drink car YES!! RED DRINK CAR YES!!!!!"

This was repeated ad nauseum all the way home at full throttle screaming volume.

10th May 2012
Spoken language / understanding

7.45pm
We are on our usual Thursday evening drive.
H agitated: "D M... D M... get D M...?"
Me: "D M? Where's the DM? On the game?" He is playing his ipod
game – naturally.
H, calmer, stating: "D M."
Me: "Oh... D M... right... !" (??!)
Yeah I know, I'm just going to repeat stuff and go with it!

8.45pm
About to change H's nappy before bed.
"G coonan..."
Me: G coonan?"

What?!?
Again, I'm just gonna repeat stuff…

13th May 2012
More OCD...?

We are on the way home from the play barn. We've got the
obligatory helium balloon in the car.
"Help balloon!!"
Oh dear, it can't be completely symmetrical or something. The knot
is leaning to one side which means the balloon when resting against
the car roof is on the wonk.
I pull the ribbon down a bit so it's straight.

"Hand off!"
I let go of the balloon, it goes wonky again.
This pattern is repeated for the next five minutes, interspersed with
me taking it into the front with me and surreptitiously tying it to the
handle of my bag to hold it straight. But then of course it's not
touching the roof as it should.

Oh dear.

Lots of sleight of hand later (me sneakily holding the balloon) and swift distraction with the phone game and we are ok again.

On the way home we pick up G from his carer's. All is fine. We set off again.

"Mummy help!!"

Me: "Where do you want the help?"

H: "That there" pointing at the windscreen.

This is repeated to increasing levels of distress as we stop the car again and I rub at the lights, visor and windscreen all to no avail.

Me: "It's fine! There's no need to help!! Show Mummy where you want the help!"

I unclip his seatbelt so he can come in the front to show me. That's not good enough.

H is now really distressed: "Seatbelt on!!"

I clip him in again.

"Help that there!!!" Here we go again.

We have put both the visors up in case that was it.

"Down!!!"

I am trying to see where he is pointing from his viewpoint when I see the visors aren't quite level.

Oh boy.

I move the passenger side visor a fraction of an inch.

Wow. Magic.

A quick spin through his calming down ritual of "dry your eyes, cuddle..." etc and all is quiet again.

15th May 2012
I don't do mornings!!

Took the chance last night to try and get at least some decent kip by taking a sleeping tablet.

H has been in my bed since 1am-ish as usual.

5.30am

H, half asleep: "Neck under."

Me, can't really speak properly yet: "Hmmm?"
H, louder: "Neck under."
Me: "Und..."
H: "Neck under!!"
Me: "Neckunder..."

A moment later...
H: "Arms under."
Me: "Mmm."
H: "H arms under!"
Me: "H-ar-z-und..."

Both half asleep and I've still gotta parrot what he says...

17th May 2012
Trees have feelings too...

Coming out of school we see a girl attempting to climb a tree.
"Climb tree girl."
Me: "Yes the girl is climbing the tree."
We walk on by.
H stops and turns around. He has his fist raised with his index finger crooked out to point.
"Be careful tree..."
Another step then turns around again...
"Tree broken... wipe your eyes tree... it's all right tree... tree is fine..."

19th May 2012
A varied diet...

So five days ago G had a real thing for southern fried breaded chicken pops. Couldn't get enough, so I went out and bought 3 more packets. Cooked some last night and he didn't touch them.
Oh well.

This morning he'd been in the garden, Steve found him with what looked like snot smeared all round his mouth. G then calmly carried on dipping his finger into the snail shell he was holding and... well you can guess the rest.

19th May 2012
Word association / brand recognition

I turn the telly on and there is a diamond jubilee thing on with the Queen having the national anthem sung to her.
I tell H that's the Queen.
H: "Queen... crown."
A minute later...
"Queen... Burger King!"

Hmm... hungry?

20th May 2012
Helpful husband!

So I've had a bit of a lie-in as Steve is here entertaining the boys. H comes upstairs to find me.
"Mummy get bubble anti-nate" – at least that's what it sounds like.
Eh?

We go downstairs to investigate ("Show Mummy the bubble anti-nate") and I see there is a new Facebook game that has been added to my profile called Bubble Atlantis.
Oh.

Later on Steve comes in. He tells me he thought H might like that game. I re-acquaint him with the fact that every morning H already has to play two bubble pop games before we can leave for school. I generally try to sneak myself on to the computer to ditch most of the lives on the games so it won't take so long, but H seems to be getting wise to this.
Now he will have 3 games to play.

Thank you very much husband!

21st May 2012
I… have no idea..?

H: "Nappy mono…"

Huh?

23rd May 2012
Difficulty functioning

So it's Wednesday today.
Friday night when Steve was back was supposed to be a catch up.
Unfortunately G thought it was quite nice to get up before 3am.
Saturday and Sunday night I got four to five hours sleep, though to be fair I did go back to bed Saturday morning for an hour or so.
Monday night I was really flagging so cancelled going to a friend's leaving drinks and took a sleeping tablet instead. Cue G getting up at 3.45am.
Tuesday: failure to get to sleep in the day and an appointment with choir in the evening require me to swill down a caffeine tablet with copious amounts of Pepsi Max. Steve gets back from work at 11.30pm, he;s got a bit of leave.
I go into G's room again and actually get almost 6 hours.

Bizarrely my best kip of the week leaves me feeling totally wrecked today and really finding it difficult to function.
How does that work?!

23rd May 2012
Behaviour: H

We are in the garden. The boys are on and off the trampoline and climbing frame etc. H is getting increasingly "hands on" with G.
I tell him repeatedly not to touch G, to give G space, be nice to G etc. They are back on the trampoline when despite my warnings H

looks at me and starts hitting G on the back. I then promptly drag him off the trampoline and hustle him to his room.

H demands his disk – I tell him no. Frankly I've had enough as I am way too tired at this point.

Full meltdown follows; I'm in tears as well – fun times!

Later when things are calm again H keeps saying "Mummy fierce."
I didn't think I was that bad considering!

Chapter 7

Death by rituals

Respite

I feel I need to say something about this.

Respite is not easily won, and yes, I'm afraid it may be a postcode lottery on who gets it, or a case of "the squeakiest wheel gets the oil." I am very lucky to get the level of support I do at the moment. I know I'm lucky, because it took years to get to this point! It's actually not easy to ask for help; after all, I went into motherhood with my eyes as open as they can be!

It was always my intention to be a stay at home Mum; everybody has to make their own choice, and after two rounds of IVF that was mine. Steve and I were both agreed on this. They were our boys, we should be able to provide for them ourselves shouldn't we? Steve had a good job, I'm at home...

In the end though I got better at letting people see past the happy / manic facade ("it's fine really!!!") and slowly got more support.

And thank goodness, as having more help at home as well as overnight respite for the boys probably saved my sanity! The personal assistants that have helped us in our home, as well as volunteers from the Forces charity SSAFA, have all been a wonderful help. The couple that have G for overnight care have become like surrogate Grandparents to him, and Annie, helping me at home through some very tough times while Steve has been working away has become a close family friend.

Family have been great too. Though they are not local to us they help where they can. Sadly my own Mum passed away the year before I had G, so she wasn't around to help me or answer Mum type questions. My in-laws were great though, letting us come to stay so that we could have a "holiday" in their house, with the extra helping hands they provided. Steve's sister too would often visit at these times to give extra help; as well as opening up her own home to us in the summer holidays.

That's about it really; but as you read on I just wanted you to know that all these people were helping me, yet it was still really, really hard. I know of so many people that struggle yet don't get the help I do.

24th May 2012
Extended bedtime ritual

H has a toy in bed: Big Pooh or Big Dog. I have to repeat everything H says.
So when we put H to bed it goes as follows:

Radio or disk on (delete as applicable).
H: "Big Pooh arms is under."
Me: ditto.
H: "Big Pooh neck is under."
Me: ditto.
H then leaves his arms outside of the duvet. "Cat rug."
I place cat rug over his arms.
H: "H arms is under."
Me: ditto.
H: "H neck is under."
Me: ditto.
H: "Night Mummy."
Me: ditto, then I wave.
H: "Waving Mummy."
Me: ditto.
H: "Night H. Waving H." (Waves.)
Me: ditto.
I go out and shut the door.

Once I'm outside the door H generally says "H arms under / neck under" (notice the absence of the word 'is' this time.) Then "H eyes closed" which I, naturally, have to repeat.

He is doing this a lot lately: saying stuff that he expects me to repeat when I'm not in the room. Unfortunately I don't have Superman calibre hearing so my lack of response often causes distress.
I have now learnt to hang around outside his bedroom door waiting for the inevitable parroting session.

27th May 2012
Being included (against my will!) in H's rituals

Today, the things I have had to do to avert cataclysmic meltdowns from H include:
Getting dressed before being allowed to undress again to get in the bath;
Making Steve unlock one door from inside as H refused to let us go in the perfectly good, open other door;
Laying down, taking my glasses off then putting them on again;
Endlessly repeating nonsensical phrases.

29th May 2012
Making a stand... or not...

So I had a multi-agency meeting today about G, though we are now starting to discuss H as well, as our family kind of comes as a package.
I have mentioned some of the issues surrounding H's controlling behaviour and anxiety, and it was agreed that when we move house it would be a good time to try and break some of the rituals; especially the bedtime parroting.
I decided to test this out a little by not repeating H saying "H get phone game on."
Five minutes later H is screaming the words into my face with tears rolling down his own. We then have the usual bout of leaping up and

banging down on his knees, scraping his wrists across the carpet, whacking his head with his hands.

I end up having to lie down, glasses off (tried to refuse this one but had them ripped off my face anyway) eyes closed, Mummy sleep (and yes we have to do snoring noises), cuddle.

We have to do all this 3 times.

Think until I get some practical advice on how to handle this I'll go back to being controlled...

29th May 2012
Touchy feely

Well this is new.

Annie took the boys to the playground tonight, H was walking. On the way there and back he was wanting to touch everything: the trees, the lampposts, bending down to touch the grass, wanting to kick the piles of grass where it had been cut recently.

He has been running his hands over car bonnets that we pass walking back from school for some time, but not wanting to touch *everything*.

30th May 2012
You want to go back to work? Err... no!

The OT asked me again yesterday if I would consider going back to work instead of Steve when he finishes the RAF in January. I didn't think so: I mean I haven't been in work, apart from helping out for a couple of hours in the Thrift shop since getting pregnant with G.

Yesterday morning G was up from 3 to 5am.

Today he got up at 3am. H got up at 5.30am and did his Jedi mind thing of making me talk myself slowly insane by repeating everything three times over.

This was on top of consistently getting less than four decent hours kip a night for the last few weeks.

Taking H to school was a challenge; windows down, concentrating hard, the drive was ok. Dragging my arse out of the car was not so easy: felt like my arms and legs were twice their size and weight - that's saying something! I could have happily laid down on the ground in a sunny spot and drifted off through sheer exhaustion.

Back home after a late breakfast / exceedingly early lunch I crash out upstairs. Despite the alarm going off when it's time to get H I feel myself constantly fighting being dragged down to that dark comfy place inside...

So why then, when asked if I would go back to work do I forget the bleeding obvious... when the heck would I *ever* sleep?!!

1st June 2012
Communicating

"Boat to the Granddad's house."
??
"Car to the Granddad's house."
"We're not going to Granddad's house!"
"Car to Granddad's house picture!"
I think this refers to something on Facebook. There is a picture of four people on a train that I suppose could remind him of the ferry we went on last year to see Steve's sister. The seats look similar. We came back from Jersey on the ferry then stayed at Granddad's house. Ok, could make sense.

"Boat to the windmill!"

Nope. Don't know what that means!

4th June 2012
Language / Perception of words?

H has had a poo.
Me: "H have new nappy."
H: "Nappy... Scrabble shirt!"

I dunno… he has seen me playing a Scrabble game on the computer and happens to be wearing a shirt that says "Soccer crew" on it...?

6th June 2012
Knackered

Last night I was late going to bed... ok, ok I know that's not unusual and it's my own damn fault for being an insomniac! Anyway, H has started crying in his room before I've even gone up, so I go into his room.

"Disk off, Mummy's room." He is pretty adamant about this and is getting pretty stressed so I let him go into my bed. He sparks out again and I follow suit after 10 minutes or so. It's now half past midnight.

I doze off. Next thing I know G's door alarm has gone off. Feels like I've been asleep a while; I look at the time; I haven't. It's 1am.

G has wandered off downstairs so I grab him, plus a drink and take him back to his room, laying down next to him. He's a little active but not too noisy, so I'm not sure what time we both nod off.

3am
Oh good. H has come in to find us. I hustle him into my room with me and into bed, hoping not to disturb G. G follows. Damn!
I get G back to his room again.
Sadly I can't really sleep very well after this.

5am
H is awake and ready to start the day. Lovely. There's an expression: "eyes like pissholes in the snow." I'm pretty sure that's what I must look like.

We go downstairs after about half an hour. It actually takes me a few minutes to notice that G is asleep on the sofa. I obviously forgot to re-set the door alarm after I put him back at 1am.

Not feeling that alert today to be honest.
I feel another day of tea, Pepsi Max and caffeine tablets coming on.

9th June 2012
Really inappropriate

In the car, hubby is driving and H and I are in the back. H pulls me across for a cuddle.
Me: "You want cuddle?"
H: "Tongue!"
"Tongue? H that's funny!"
I try to sit up.
"Mummy tongue!"
He's got me around the neck, I know what he wants here as he tried to do it once before... he is trying to put his mouth to mine, and touch his tongue to mine.
Yes I know, disturbing!

"H we don't do that."
"Kiss tongue!!" Oh dear just wrong on so many levels!
"H that's not right we don't kiss tongues!!!"
He's getting rather agitated; he desperately wants me to put my tongue out...
Steve suggests I put my finger on my tongue and transfer a "kiss" that way, sort of...
I do this, he is still trying to "kiss tongue." I say it's a rule we don't kiss tongues.
He is still a little agitated but I keep saying "H that's not right, you are funny!"
After a few minutes he seems to accept this.
Thank goodness.

9th June 2012
Human dictaphone

H is talking me to death again, wanting me to parrot him. I'm tired and I'm just not in the mood. I am trying not to give in to it but I'm afraid resistance is futile.
Cue the following phrases that I end up having to say: (in ever increasing volume I'm afraid...)
"Mummy want to talk..."

"Mummy doesn't want to talk!" (After I said this back!!)
"Ooh ah ah…" (Yep, just as it sounds!)
"Mummy angry."
"Shh finger."

This last one is because I'm trying to hush him; I just end up having to say "Shh finger" instead which kind of defeated the object of that one.

10th June 2012
Losing a tooth

H has had two wobbly front teeth for a while.
It's the weekend so Steve gets the honour of sharing the bed with H. On waking in the morning H presents Steve with one of his front teeth.
"Bedcat tooth!!"
Remember this is the cat bolster that lies in the bed at night to stop H flopping all over us.
Steve asks has he got his other tooth.
H simply grins at Steve and wobbles his tooth with his tongue.
No meltdowns, no requests to "fix the tooth."

A surprisingly pain-free experience!

11th June 2012
Turning into the sort of parent you always said you'd never be…

Getting REALLY fed up with the whole having to parrot H thing now…
Phoned up an automated message of cinema times, only to have to re-dial 3 times before I actually heard it.
I've got the phone pressed hard against my head but all I can hear is an increasingly agitated and screechy H trying to prompt me to copy him.
He is sat at the computer, about to play a game.

His language goes something like this: "H can move the chair... click yes... phone game flag finished... *H get phone game flag finished!!!*"
After my third interrupted call to the cinema I am feeling rather stroppy.

My language goes something like this:
"Mummy doesn't want to talk... be quiet please! ... phone game flag off... Whatever H! Leave me alone... Mummy wants to be quiet... *for fuck's sake!!!!*"
Yep. I know.
Now I'm one of those horrible adults that scream obscenities at their children.
And a disabled child at that.
Great isn't it.

11ᵗʰ June 2012
Trying to stop the whole parroting thing... baby steps...

After the above incident and the inevitable meltdown that followed, H decided he didn't want the computer on after all. He wants the phone game again.
"Mummy get 3 squares."
This means 3 notches on the volume. I change the volume, but don't say anything.
"Mummy get 3 squares!!"
Me: "Yes I've done it!" (Showing him the volume setting.)
H: "I've done 3 squares!"
Me: "That's right."
H: "I've done 3 squares?"
Me: "Good."
He wanders off, saying no more.

Like I said – baby steps.

12th June 2012
You *will* go on the swing!

I'm in the garden with the boys. Things are ok, G is going on the trampoline, closely followed by H.

G then paces round the end of the garden. I am watching him all the time as he likes to escape into the garden next to the one out the back.

H spots the swings that Steve had hooked up out of the way when cutting the grass earlier.

"H swing, Mummy push H swing!"

Ok that's fine.

"G swing!"

Here's the thing, G doesn't want to go on the swing. I know what's coming (damn it!) so I try to coax G over. I know, that was probably a mistake too as now H thinks I've sanctioned it somehow. When you're tired and trying to avert disaster the decisions you make on the spur of the moment aren't always sensible ones.

Ok so G is at the swing but won't sit down and skips off again.

H: "G SWING!!!"

Me: "G doesn't want to go on the swing. G playing in the garden. It's ok for G to play in the garden."

No. Not acceptable.

H leaps up into the air, tucking his feet under his bum, then slams back down on his knees. Oh God.

Full on screaming mode now. I'm not surprised, that must've hurt.

He's asking for the whole "make it better" ritual of sticker on, sticker off, kiss it better, rub it better, whilst still slapping his head.

I manage to get both boys inside.

I have to lock the back door and remove the key to stop G seizing the moment and legging it over the garden fence while I'm sorting H. I've done this and am just going into the lounge where the boys have gone when I hear the sound of two loud slaps on flesh.

I get in there and G is trying to huddle on the floor while H rips the shirt from G's back.

I just know it wasn't G hitting H and I'm afraid I go into full-on protective mother mode.

"YOU DO NOT HURT G!!! GET UPSTAIRS NOW! H'S ROOM!!!"

I'm afraid I smack his bum a couple of times; I know, I know. H goes to his room to complete the meltdown / reset cycle.

Sadly whilst just now G was keeping himself to himself and had no outward sign of distress, he now bursts into tears and just looks horribly upset. This seems all the more awful as it's such a rare occurrence.

I just feel hideous.

12ᵗʰ June 2012
Annie's Story: H attack!!

Here's Annie again:

Mum has gone out to choir and Steve left shortly after her this evening after a couple of days holiday fixing up the new house. He said the usual goodbyes to H who went to bed about 9pm.

Before going to bed H had had a mini meltdown, asking for "red drink in classroom" – obviously impossible!!

As soon as Steve had left H was down the stairs.

H: "Trousers up."

Trousers were already up so I just pulled them a bit higher and proceeded to get him back to bed.

So I get upstairs and H is going on about Daddy gone, phone game flag gone etc. I just kept repeating what H said – any way to get him settled!

I close his door... then hear H run head first into it like a bull into a red cloth! BANG! I go back in where he full on hits me on my chest – OUCH!

I'm taken aback by this so I grab the DVD player and exit the room, where he hurls himself into the door a few more times. He then throws the radio. I know it's something solid from the different tone in the bang.

I walk in to get it and ask H to calm down...

He launches himself at me pushing me against the door and going for whatever bit of me he can!! At this I am in total shock, he has NEVER actually meant to hurt me like this... I exit the room quickly without saying a word... more human sounding banging, then more objects thrown.

I go back into the room to retrieve the objects.

As soon as H sees me he goes in for the attack again. This time I get hold of him and try to restrain him to calm him. It doesn't work; he is far too strong and he's really hurting me. I get him on the bed, put the duvet over him and weigh it down with pure force.

Me: "H it's bed time."

He starts to calm down, asking for disk. He is still sobbing as we go through all the normal stuff... then he gives a final blow to my arm and head, so then we have to go through the whole "sticker" routine again.

At this point I'm hurting! So after half an hour I think he is calm I can still hear him occasionally sobbing. Was this because of Daddy going back to work? Mummy going out also?

He has never directed his anger towards me physically like that before; yes the occasional hit or scratch, but usually with an immediate "sorry... hug... sticker..." etc.

What did I do wrong?!!

Annie didn't do anything wrong... keep reading...

12th June 2012
Dyslexic??

In Annie's story above:

"Before going to bed H had had a mini meltdown, asking for "red drink in classroom" – obviously impossible!!!"

The annoying thing is I know what H had meant when he said this... but I keep asking for input from speech therapy as what H means and what H says are often two different things!

Some months ago H was doing his trick of trying to read road signs... "Classroom road!"

Only because I was there when he said this did I realise he was trying to read the road sign that had the same name as the school. As far as I can work out, the school name to him looked like the word classroom.

When you do the National Autistic Society's Early Bird course they always say you need to "be a detective." Not half!!

H's new school bottle had the school's name on it in big bold letters. It also had a red drink in it. He was simply asking Annie for his drink bottle... but how on earth was she supposed to know that?!

H often muddles up letters in words: "conitue" instead of "continue" when playing computer games is a perennial favourite of his.

13th June 2012
Eh... what??

This evening H was having a minor wobble about "green drink."
OK we don't have any green drink, or green bottles.
He also kept saying "green drink classroom..."
Oh God that again...

Got the school bottles but he kept pushing them away...
Eventually I spotted a green glass bottle of cordial, that I must stress, H has NEVER had!!
I took the green bottle in one hand, had the school bottle in the other which had a bit of orange squash in it. He then ignores the green cordial, grabs the orange squash and drinks it down.
And yes, this same bottle was one of the ones offered before...

14th June 2012
Not coping well...

This sounds awful, but CONSTANTLY being forced to repeat every little thing, as well as running into whatever room H is in to do so is almost making me start to resent him.

I especially feel this way as I don't like the fishwife I become when it gets to me too much, which in turn makes G flee for a quiet space.

H's behaviour feels like it's dominating every aspect of our home life... when does G get any of my time?!

This evening H had a mini-meltdown (mini is good!!) because I wouldn't force G back into the car just so I could put his seatbelt on before taking it off again to go inside – all to satisfy H's obsessive rituals!

14th June 2012
Translation

"Mummy open the door" seems to translate as "get your butt in here *right* now and repeat after me..."

Sorry H... it's been a long day... coming...

14th June 2012
A different bedtime approach: thumbs up

Just did H's bedtime routine. He asked for book around 8.40pm, which I read pretty much in a monotone. (I've had enough today!)

Cleaned teeth, sat on toilet etc.

He lay down in bed where I covered him with the duvet. I turned the DVD on, saying nothing. The disk was an ABC disk.

H: "Castle, shapes, art disk."

I go to get the case of disks from the landing. By the time I find the disk he has repeated this in ever increasing stress tones 4 times. I say nothing, but point to the label of the disk.

He reads the title: "Castle, shapes art."

I give him a thumbs up.

H: "Cat rug." I *was* going to try and go without – rats!

I put the cat rug over him, at which point he asks for big dog, the huge soft toy.

I get the dog and tuck it in.

H then starts his spiel that I'm usually forced to copy to avoid meltdown:

"Big dog arms is under, big dog neck is under... H arms is under, H neck is under..."

I keep giving him a smiling thumbs up, amazingly, he doesn't force the issue...!!

H: "Bye Mummy, waving Mummy, bye H, waving H..."

I'm stood there grinning like a loon, waving with my right hand and giving a thumbs up with my left – and he's going for it!!

Asks for cuddle and kiss, that's ok.

The next bit is hard to avoid...

H: "H close eyes, Mummy get H close eyes!"

I have to run my hands over his face but I still don't say anything...

Then we are "waving Mummy..." etc again, but I'm still waving with my thumb up, that's ok.

Just about to go...

H: "Mummy sleep... Mummy sleep!!!"

Me: "Mummy not sleeping yet, Mummy sleep later!"

He mutters this after me and I close the door.

That was 10 minutes ago... fingers crossed it lasts!!

15th June 2012
Mental torture

Ok, the whole using gestures thing didn't translate to this morning.

I have had to say the following a few times before getting downstairs:
"H neck is under, H arms is under, Mummy arms is under, Mummy neck is under, Bedcat arms is under, Bedcat neck is under."

When I wanted to go downstairs H wasn't ready, so insisted I lie down and say everything again before I could get up.

Next he plays a game on the computer:
"H play Purble Place, H can move the chair, H can get move the chair, click the church, Mummy click 'yes'..." He actually wants me to click the mouse for him.

My patience is fast running out. I am trying to give smiling thumbs up instead of parroting him, but it's not working. H is escalating fast.

I have walked away. H pushes the chair over, wanting to get into the ritual of help the chair, fix the chair etc.

I say "Upstairs!" and usher him up. He goes, screaming "Disk!!"

We then have to do the whole bed routine again.

Meanwhile the bus escort has come to get G. When the screaming and banging intensifies I hand her G's shoes to put on and hustle upstairs.

"Hurt your head!! Sticker head! Sticker head off, kiss it better, rub it better..."

Have now ordered some "talking tins" - will try anything now! These are little tins that you can record and playback 10 seconds of speech. I'm hoping I can somehow get H into using them on himself instead of using me.

Things are feeling a bit desperate now. I am in a horrible dream where I am forced to narrate every detail, word and sound of H's life... also it's not enough to be in a different room and say stuff any more.

I'm not quite sure where poor G fits into this as H's controlling behaviour is swallowing everything else whole right now!

I'm finding this really difficult now, seem to be crying on a daily basis; though thankfully not usually in front of the kids!

This actually does feel like mental torture...

15th June 2012
A different bedtime approach: day 2

Well we had more waving, grinning and thumbs up; seemed to go ok. Had to say "H close eyes", then go back in to say "Mummy sleeping later."

Then another trip back up as he wanted me to move the cat rug.

I'm hoping that's it.

The waving / no talking thing is still limited to bed time. I can't fob him off with gestures during the day, but if I can persevere with bedtimes and get that sorted it will be something!

16th June 2012
A bit of respite

G was at the carers, so Annie came along to the beach for the day to help out with H.

I had a lovely afternoon reading to the sound of the high tide tumbling the stones, then later on sat in the sun plopping stones into the sea with H and Annie.

It was nice to sit still for a bit with my boy, remembering my childhood seaside holidays.

17th June 2012
Constant moving and talking

H is awake: it's a bit after 6am.
H: "H get phone game pod."
Me: "H get fo-gay pod." (I'm really tired, ok?!)
H: "H can get phone game pod."
Me: "H can get fo-game pod."
He gets up. Goes to the door.
H: "H go downstairs get phone game pod."
Me: "H go downstairs get phone game pod."
Goes downstairs. Comes back up.
"Mummy get move the phone game pod."

Oh great, this is new. Sometimes I get "Mummy open the door" – meaning; come out to the landing so you can repeat after me "H hold the rail."

Me: "H get move the phone game pod!"
H: "Mummy get move the phone game pod!!!"
A couple more recitals of this with H getting more stressed, and we go downstairs.
We look at the phone game where it is plugged in.
H points approximately 1 inch to the side of where it is laying.
Me: "Really??!!"

I move the phone game to where his finger is pointing, at which point he is happy to unplug it and take it back upstairs.

9 am

I've been lying on the sofa trying to restore some energy. I've got to get G from the carers later, I'll be on my own so God knows what I'm going to do with the boys. Thought I could go to the seaside and walk the prom; one in the buggy and one on the reins, swapping over if need be. Trouble is H is obsessed with the "slide race" (the big slippery dip slide) down by the fairground. I can't exactly go on that with him and leave G unattended at the bottom so that's a no-go, and not going on the slide would cause a meltdown, so that's not good either.

Same with the woods: would have to go to the playground there, but H needs close monitoring due to his tendency to shove little toddlers down the slide when they are taking too long. G needs monitoring due to escape tendencies.

Anyway, I digress.

H has been lying on me on the sofa, which you think would be nice. He has however been constantly wriggling, digging his heels into my shins, grabbing my head with his hand, grinding his head against mine so I'm cricking my neck as I dangle off the edge of the pillow. He is playing the phone game all the while.

Later...

I have got up and am typing up some stuff on the computer, H is watching "The Chase" – his favourite quiz show.

He is constantly pacing up and down, saying stuff like "H watching The Chase!" I am expected to repeat this several times, I'm obviously not getting the nuances right.

Me: "H sit down watch The Chase." He sits.

H: "H watching The Chase." Yes we have to go through that again.

I go back to the hallway to the computer. The door is always open.

H: "Mummy open the door!"

He does this a lot. Sometimes I'm up and down like a fricking yo-yo.

Me: "H, Mummy is here! H watch The Chase!"

H: "Mummy open the door!!!"

I go in. He crooks his finger at the telly.

"H watching The Chase!"

Me: "H watching The Chase."

H: "H watching The Chase.

Me: "H watching The Chase! Mummy doesn't want to talk any more!" Gritted teeth, getting really fed up now.
H: "H watching The Chase!!"
Me: "H watching The Chase H watching The Chase H watching The Chase H WATCHING THE CHASE!!"

Yep I'm afraid I lost it.
He starts to hit me then smacks himself on the head... then, oh God... wait for it... wait for it...
He screams, leaps up and then slams down on his knees.
Me: *"It's all right H!!"*
"It's all right H."
We then have to go through the usual ritual of calming him down.

A few minutes later:
H: "Wipe your eyes." I give him a tissue. He cuddles me, then pulls back, smiling:
"*So* gorgeous!!!"
Me: ditto.
H: "SO much!!!" He's taken this from me saying "I love you SO much!!"
He resumes pacing up and down, intermittently sitting on the sofa half upside-down.

I'm really struggling at the moment... but I do love that boy.

Chapter 8

Up and down

Phew, still struggling to keep upbeat... thank heavens for the friends I have to offload to... I have friends within the local support group who all know how difficult it can be. Sanity is preserved by getting out as often as possible for tea, bacon butties, cake, whatever takes your fancy. I don't know about you, but a cheese scone perks me up no end.

17th June 2012
Thumbs up

Just since this morning I have introduced the thumbs up / no speaking system.
This only works when it's something he obviously just wants repeated, as opposed to a request. (Did I say request? I meant instruction!!)
He's mostly going with it, though he is pushing for a reaction, saying multiple times "H's a good boy!" before letting it drop.

19th June 2012
Talking tins

Well I ordered some talking tins and they've arrived, they can record up to 10 seconds of audio. Bearing in mind H will make a ritual out of something after I've done it once, I'm a little wary. I've just done "H's a good boy" with the idea that instead of me having to be in his sight all the time to do the thumbs up he can have me talking to him.
He's re-playing it over and over again - will see how much peace it buys me!

Hmm... now he wants *me* to press the recording... not quite what I was going for... kind of defeats the object...

I've now hidden the talking tin as it was fast becoming another phase of the ritual! Back to the drawing board.

19th June 2012
Trying to make the most of the night-time...

10.45pm
Cheese and bickies and a zopiclone chaser; yum yum! It's a bit late for a sleeping tablet I know, but I'm making the most of my last G-free night!!
He has been away with school for a 2 night break and will be back tomorrow.
Bless him, it will be good to have him back tomorrow, though I can't deny it has been easier...!

20th June 2012
Verbal stimming?

I have been researching bits on the internet (I know, probably not a good idea!!) and was reading an article about stimming. This is short for self-stimulation; can be hand flapping, spinning, etc.

I'm not sure if H's repeating would be classed as stimming, or just a ritual? Now I have managed to stop myself from having to verbally repeat everything by giving him thumbs up, things have changed a little.

H immediately latched on to the thumbs up sign by saying "H's at good boy!" Now he is constantly doing the talking for both of us:

"H have a sweet." Thumbs up.

"H's at good boy!" (Yes that *is* how he says it.)

"H orange oranges flavour sweet." Thumbs up.

"H's at good boy!"

"H eating sweet." Thumbs up.

"H's at good boy!"

We sometimes get a double-up:

"H take your left shoe off, H take your right shoe off, H's at good boy, H's at good boy!"

"H's at good boy" is always said in precisely the same sing-songy tone.

20ᵗʰ June 2012
G Force

Ahh... I have my lovely boy back again, he skipped straight by my waiting   arms   into   the   kitchen...!
Still, we have had our deep pressure hugs and now he has taken himself off to his room. Probably quite like a normal 11 year old then?!

21ˢᵗ June 2012
Repeating vs. Thumbs up – standoff

Annie reported last night while I was out that H is getting increasingly "twitchy" with the whole thumbs up things in the evenings. He seems to be extending the ritual to compensate for the lack of Annie repeating him.

During the bedtime routine he's telling her to close the door, open the door again. He will yell at her when she thinks he's finished and has gone downstairs, just to go in the room and have him tell her he's yawned, or is tired. She had to go up around 30 times to respond to these screams.

In the end she resorted to going back to the repeating to calm him down which seemed to work.

21st June 2012
G Force the healer!

Well things have been hovering just under crisis point for nearly 2 months now... since BLACK Friday!! It's been particularly difficult again today as we've gone back to the repeating instead of doing thumbs up as this was just making H even *more* stressy.

H started a meltdown earlier on the way home because I was trying not to repeat *everything*. Since getting home he's banged his knees down several times, once on concrete; he's had me read his bedtime book twice and I've subsequently had to get into my bed with him each time. After a while if I say I'm getting up he freaks out, makes me get back into bed, go through all the usual repeating: then says "Mummy getting up" or "Mummy getting downstairs."

I was lying there feeling really trashed through not enough sleep, with a bad headache that I haven't been able to shift all day. I started to feel quite sorry for myself (man up woman!!) and had a few tears.

Then G comes in, my beautiful G: he lays his body over mine and is smiling into my eyes as he giggles uncontrollably. I'm always in awe of the amazing power of G Force cuddles!

I squeeze him really hard and kiss his smiling cheeks and tell him over and over that I love him.

After a few minutes he has stopped giggling. He vocalizes "oo oof" very softly, then moves away after a moment to go and play with my feet.

I wonder what he was trying to say.

22nd June 2012
Oh God what now?!!!!

So as well as wanting me to repeat everything H thinks my hands should be tools for his own use. He is trying desperately to get me to press the various buttons on his phone game.
I won't let him. I don't fancy another thing for him to obsess over.
He escalates quickly but I'm sticking to my guns, trying to get him to do it himself.

He is desperately trying to get me to repeat stuff, which I am doing at the moment, and to do stuff, which I'm not.
Slams down on his knees, scrapes his wrists, screams, hits me in the chest.
Any time he hits me he gets sent upstairs to his room.
He balks on the landing screaming "Hug!!"
Me: "Calm down in room then hug."
He's really quite out of it now, still screaming in my face yelling "Downstairs!"
I again say room first then downstairs. I manage to get him to his bed, he's pretty much beside himself at this point.
I lie down with him as he wants me to "sleep" saying as little as possible. I've taken my glasses off as per H's demands but am still silent – he then punches me in the face.
Ok I'm up, I'm up!!
"You do *not* hit Mummy you stay in your room and calm down!!"
I hold the bedroom door closed.
I hear repeated body slams and punching of furniture, walls and door. This is terrible. I'm worried he'll do himself an injury so take him downstairs.
He proceeds to do more knee slamming. I'm worried about his knees now so I stick him on the sofa and pin the blanket over his arms as he is constantly trying to punch himself in the head and face.
After a few minutes he starts saying "It's ok H" which I repeat. Also "Sticker knee, rub knee..." I don't actually need to put a "sticker" (plaster) on now, I just do the actions.
He still keeps relapsing into head slapping etc and hits me in the chest.
I've had enough. I'm now in tears.

H: "Wipe your eyes!!!"

He is screaming this now, I wipe my eyes but don't speak, despite him trying to pull my mouth open to make me say the words.

He then randomly asks for Twinkle Twinkle Little Star music. I start singing it but I'm tired and upset so only manage the first 2 lines. He then prompts me to sing each subsequent line until I'm finished – we are both sobbing the words through our tears now!!

After this I am able to get the weighted jacket on him for 10 minutes. This was given to us by the OT.

He then says "Pants off." I take his trousers off at which point we have to rub and kiss better his knees several times, then go to wash them in the bathroom.

They are looking rather red and ever so slightly grazed by the carpet.

I'm still not repeating anything and we've gone back to me giving the thumbs up and H saying "H's at good boy."

So that's something.

24th June 2012
Groundhog Day ain't got nothing on this

Bedtime.

Cleaning teeth.

We have successfully cleaned teeth to the tune of here we go round the mulberry bush: "This is the way we brush our teeth."

H stops, turns back to me and says "Toothpaste... Ahhh... Eeee..."

Oh I see. Annie said he was doing this with her more, making her do the different mouth shapes and sounds.

After trying the thumbs up for this I do the sounds. Not good enough. "Toothpaste!" H then proceeds to get quite stressed, making me put the toothpaste lid on and off and put more on the brush.

He prompts me to start brushing teeth: "This is the way..." then stops me. Cue more toothpaste, more ahhh and eee sounds, more stressing, more toothpaste lid on and off...

We end up with around 8 attempts before I get it right.

Fast-forward to getting in bed.

H has a combo of around 12 to 15 phrases that he likes to use once he's in bed.

He says one, I do thumbs up. This is actually an improvement on me precisely repeating everything he says trust me! For each phrase he's uttered he must say "H's at good boy."

During the last 45 minutes of trying to get him to settle I think I have heard "H's at good boy" around 300 times.

Not so much re-living one day as re-living the same 5 minutes over and over.

** After consulting with Annie on this it turns out she always says Wipe your mouth" on the towel... I've never said this, but it now appears H is combining different rituals.

Note: Since this incident, after saying all the "H's at good boys" H now says a final "Really good boy H!"
This is because Annie praised him hugely after managing to get H to use his own hands (with prompting) instead of hers. Now he has incorporated this into his rituals too.

25th June 2012
Mood vs. Food

So this morning my shopping consisted of a bottle of port and a bottle of dessert wine. Think I might need some chocolate...

28th June 2012
Day off school

Today is a teacher training day allowing people to take their kids to the Norfolk show.

It's really hot and muggy and we've been awake a while.

H has had a mini paddy after I refused to pick his book up off the floor and asked him to do it. We have the usual banging down on the knees.

20 minutes later we have been up to bed, arms tucked under etc before I'm finally allowed to go downstairs again. H follows bringing the iPad.

"H crying picture."
There is a Dali-esque self-portrait photo on the screen.
Me: "H's not crying, there's no tears!"
"H hurt knees picture."

28th June 2012
G 'singing'

Have only really noticed 2 different tunes before... and only a couple of phrases: "Frere Jacques" and "London bridge is falling down." (London bridge is falling down, falling down, falling down, London bridge is falling down, falling down, falling down etc. Note we don't get to "My fair lady...")
Today we had a complete rendition of "Row, row, row your boat", or in G's words:
"Ooh ah doig-a doig..." (gently down the stream...)

28th June 2012
MASSIVE meltdown on Annie's watch

I went out to an evening support meeting. This is what happened while I was out.

Annie had the boys at the Thrift shop, where I then left them to go out to my meeting.
Possible triggers:
It was a really hot, muggy day.
G got fed up in the Thrift shop and pulled Annie's hair. H seemed ok with it, just said "Poor Marianne."
H then tripped over when walking home - seemed to get over it with the usual rituals of "rub it better" etc.

At home H has a tub of food to eat.
H: "Peppers and grapes and cucumber and orange."
Annie initially didn't repeat 'properly' missing out a couple of "ands."
Annie: "Peppers, grapes, cucumber and orange."
She was soon 'corrected' though and H carried on eating.

Annie prepares a toasted hot cross bun; this is not unusual.
H then asked for "warm toast." This is what I had given him for tea earlier.
H then threw the hot cross bun...

He then threw everything off the table, jumped and banged down onto his knees and banged his head. Did this a couple of times quite badly, Annie tried to stop him harming himself.

H headbutted Annie, she sent him to his room to calm down. We have made a point of putting him in his room when he deliberately hurts one of us, to try and point out it's unacceptable.

She could hear him headbutting and hitting everything in the room so brought him out.
H then continued the knee and head banging and scraping his wrists on the carpet.
After coming downstairs, H deliberately bangs his pointed toes into the floor quite hard: "Hurt toes."

Annie phones me after unsuccessfully trying to calm H down for 45 minutes.

At this point Annie noticed a bite mark on H's upper arm, assumed he did this while in his room. He is picking up items and biting them really hard – a kid's fruit drink bottle, an empty crisp packet etc. He tries to bite Annie's knee; she sends him back to his room.

She hears a couple of big bangs so brings him downstairs again. H is stripping his own clothes off as they are doing this.
The usual ritual of "Sticker on, rub it better, kiss it better..." etc has not been working the whole time.

Around an hour and a quarter after he started H appears to be wearing himself out. Annie sits in the room with H and ignores him while this is happening except when he starts asking for the calming ritual ("rub it better" etc) again. Around this time a friend has arrived at my request to take G out and entertain him for a bit to help Annie until I can get back home.

Annie is able to dab water on H's head now as a lump has come up.
He strips his nappy off so Annie is able to put a new one on and put
him in pyjamas.
She gives him some paracetamol as she is worried he must be hurting
after all the self-abuse.

3rd July 2012
Phantom loo roll nicker

Keep going to the toilet forgetting to check for loo roll: it's not a
good look to waddle over to the airing cupboard with your knickers
round your ankles.
Thank you G for nicking the paper again.
When I come out of the loo I find him chewing on an ancient
denture cleaning tablet that used to belong to my Mum. I now use
them for cleaning the toilet so probably not the tastiest thing to suck
on.

3rd July 2012
Stuck in the staying in bed ritual

Reduced to tears by a 7 year old boy again.
Not much else to say really.

Chapter 9

More medication... where's my share?!

My drugs? Well I'm stockpiling sleeping tablets for when we go on holiday to my Sister-in-law's place. They are fab at helping us and taking them out for walks and stuff, so it's a good chance to catch up on some quality kip... I hope! We've also been really lucky that both the boys have been selected to go on the SSAFA holiday for disabled kids. SSAFA is a forces charity. G has been before but this has been the first time H has been old enough to go. G loved it, loads of activities, so I'm hoping H will too.
Oh, and we will be child-free for 5 nights!!

3rd July 2012
H starting melatonin

This evening we started H on Circadin, the cheaper tablet form of melatonin. We have to crush the tablets that say do not crush, as they are meant to be slow release, but hey-ho.

He had had another paddy so asked for book early anyway, I went to choir and Annie only had to repeat the bedtime ritual once.

I think he'd cried himself out and was pretty tired anyway to be honest.

Still got up in the night though – I didn't really expect anything else!

July 2012
More drugs! ADHD alert

G's behaviour had taken a bit of a downturn alongside H's, though not in such a spectacular fashion. We had all the spitting and attitude. Maybe this is quite normal for a lad his age...?
At one of the multi-agency meetings the school told me he had been quite difficult there too, gleefully running around on the tables at school. Ok maybe that's not quite regular behaviour...
Shortly after this both the school and I filled in the Conners questionnaire.
Result: probable ADHD.
Oh good! Well he's always been on the move, that's just G.

The paediatrician decided to double his dose of Risperidone, as he was on quite a low dose. This did really help, fingers crossed it will stay that way for the time being.
Nobody wants to medicate their kids but it just helps his concentration and mood, he is definitely still our cheeky G!

4th July 2012
Night time antics

2am: G kicked-off for a bed bouncing marathon. I was then woken from a combat kip by the lovely aroma of discarded nappy at 5.30am - cue emergency bath.
It's going to be a long day.

On the plus side I have been "allowed" to get out of bed early by H by negotiating a 10 second countdown to getting up.

5th July 2012
A down day

The demanding, controlling behaviour was out of control again this morning so I'm afraid I really lost my patience. Lots of shouting on both sides, and lots of hitting me on H's part.

H had time out in his room, where I left him until he came out of his own accord. Lots of screaming and crashing, then he came out after a couple of minutes and continued his meltdown.

Had to sing Twinkle, Twinkle Little Star, though I wasn't crying at this point.

That came later!

After dropping H off at school I sent Annie a text saying guess what song I've just heard on the radio? "What doesn't kill you makes you stronger"!! It was meant to be a joke she could appreciate, but I guess she saw it for the cry for help it obviously was and immediately phoned me back. Cue a really emotional few hours having a cuppa with Annie and crying on the poor girl's shoulder.

I've been finding it really difficult lately; emotionally.

5th July 2012
H stuff

H looking at the "surprise" symbol in G's diary, says: "Worried." (It's a face with an open mouth.)

"Mummy open the door" actually means cross the threshold and come into the room please.

"Lid off" - can mean put the lid down on a drink bottle, or the DVD player, or to put away the pull down table on the back of the car seat. "Off" seems to have the meaning of "finished."

5th July 2012
A musical interlude

Thursday evening, there is an extra practice for choir so I take the boys along with the intention of staying half an hour before taking them back to bed.

I end up staying until 10pm.

There is initially a lot of squealing and laughing, H and G chasing each other up and down the church. I have a couple of the choir members running interference on G, escorting him around the church centre building, investigating the loos. G is grabbing anyone that'll play with him; he knows one of the altos who picks him up and shares kisses with him.

He then grabs the Musical Director's hand as she's trying to conduct us... I find the sight of G being twirled round and around by her as we all sing incredibly moving; it will stay with me for a long time... he looked so content.

H sits with his snack and plays games on his ipad.

G then finds the padre in a meeting with 3 other people and decides to join them, helping himself to the comfy chair and apparently sitting there while they do their prayers.

H meanwhile is getting tired after I have given him his melatonin tablets, so I strap him into the pushchair. We are practicing "The Lord bless you and keep you" for a church service we are to sing at – H is practically asleep in the buggy.

We go home.

By the time I put H to bed he only has the energy to get me to repeat one set of rituals.

Feeling a lot happier this evening.

That's what choir does for me.

6th July 2012
Adding more elements... help!

So yesterday morning I tried to make a cut-off point in giving in to H's demands. Meltdown followed where H gave himself a nice big bruise on his head. This morning he's obviously forgotten about all that as we are back to square one, but with even more added demands. I just went with it cos I've had 3 hours kip and I haven't got the strength!!

Around 5.30am he was yelling from his room, had to go downstairs to do book. Up again to get "Disk" then told to put disk away in H's room again, then told to go and turn disk off (which I pretend to do by going out of the room and coming back). After the book we had to clean teeth, then back into H's bed. Half an hour later I have to get the radio from my room into H's room.

Half hour after that this is what he had me do after coming into my bed:
Radio back into my room plus the usual repeating of everything, arms under, etc. He then went down to get ipad, shutting the door after him as always then yelling "Mummy open the door" so I could come out and repeat that H should hold the rail. When he comes back upstairs - same thing, but after going out to say H hold the rail I then have to go back in the room and shut the door before he comes in after me.

I know how this reads but I really don't know how to go about breaking   this   habit!!
Roll on next Thursday as I have a meeting with some professional people, hope they have some better ideas!!

10th July 2012
"Move the sleeve shirt..."

Ok have just spent the last 10 minutes shouting back at H as he yells "Move the sleeve shirt there... Mummy get move the sleeve shirt!!
Nope. Moved it up, down, sideways, tried to take it off, with H yelling all the while, plus having a headbanging session. Finally tried to turn the sleeves up, this stopped him in his tracks, so we could move on to "Sticker head on, sticker head off..."
I guess the sleeves were too long.
Never mind that he had been wearing it all day!

11th July 2012
Assume the position... the *correct* position...

So I was laying on my bed with G this evening listening to Annie put H to bed.
H: "Waving goodbye Marianne."
Annie: "Waving goodbye Marianne."

This was subsequently repeated by H and Annie in turn in varying tones, H's getting more stressed. After about 30 repetitions I'm afraid I was smothering my guffaws in a pillow at the sheer ridiculousness of the situation.

Eventually Annie successfully completes the ritual and comes to talk to me.

Apparently it's no longer the tone of voice with her, it's the position she's standing in. She felt ill last week, and in her exhaustion stood with one hand braced on the wall and the other draped over the door handle.

This position now has to be repeated precisely whilst saying the above phrase.

Happy days!

12ᵗʰ July 2012
Should've gone to Specsavers...

Had a meeting today to discuss H... speech therapist, social worker, social services OT and the learning disability nurse.

It went ok, they want to do visual supports for bedtime and also around the house, like a picture of him holding the stair rail, as he always demands I come out of bed to tell him to hold the rail etc. They're going to do me a social story for when we move into the new house too.

They also said I shouldn't allow any new rituals to creep in at this point.

Oh and CAMHS (Child and Adolescent Mental Health Services) won't look at him at the moment because it's "all the autism."

So anyway feeling geed up and full of resolve I foolishly decided to try and stop one of H's OCD ritual things after school. We had just got home and the lid on the water bottle was a bit cracked, so he was desperate for me to "help" it and put a sticker on it. I've been here before, I can't make it better and he has a meltdown anyway so I thought I might as well just tell him it's broken and get the meltdown over with.

Went off big time: I left him clipped in the car seat so I could be out of punching distance. Started to calm down a bit after about 10 minutes so we went inside. I then decided to stop the excessive repeating required when taking off H's shoes.
This didn't go down well.

So long story short he smashed a mirror and punched me in the face knocking my glasses off, lovely. Good thing they were my old pair, the nose pieces are all wonky now. I just rode it out.
After calming down a bit I decided to carry on with cutting out the repeating, I had to say the same words a different way sometimes, ie:
H: "Mummy get Bubble Witch Saga"
Me: "Oh yes, H's playing Bubble Witch Saga" etc.
Generally though he accepted me saying stuff like "That's right, yes, good boy, well done."
I really thought I'd made headway, so when I went out Annie tried to continue this. He wasn't having any of it though, so she went along with him as he was escalating fast. She thought he was ok but he then started going on about "Mummy hurt head." She wasn't sure what sparked him off again but I guess he was just remembering from earlier.
Soon after this she sent me a text saying he had ripped her glasses off and snapped them. (What is it with him and glasses?!) When I phoned her I could hear he was still very upset so I got her to put him on the phone so I could sing "Twinkle twinkle" - he asks for this now after major meltdowns.
It's just demoralizing as I thought I'd made a mini breakthrough, now in the morning I'm sure I'll be back to square one!
Haven't seen his head yet, apparently he's sporting a large lump...

13th July 2012
Asking to play!

DIARY EVENT!! G just took H's hands and was jumping up and down the lounge with him! This is quite a big deal for G as he NEVER seeks such close contact with his brother!

14th July2012
Repeating everything ad nauseum – improvement!

Since Thursday I have stuck with it on the no repeating front with mixed success.

Sometimes there are things that he just won't let go, eg:

"Lid off drink, cup holder away."

Also we still have to do it at bedtime, but I can live with that.

But amazingly I am managing to reduce the repeats quite a lot, by just responding instead. Sometimes I have to put the words he's used in, just in a different way.

Otherwise I can just say things like "good boy, that's right, well done."

It's like we had to have a total crisis about it before things could improve a little.

I'm not complaining, improvement is improvement: I really felt I was going insane with it all!

16th July 2012
Deja vu...

Ok the mostly non-repeating thing was going reasonably well, but surprise surprise after going out for a day with choir and leaving them with Steve yesterday things are back to square one! Thankfully the 2 sleeping tablets have taken the edge right off my stress levels this morning... just too knackered to care much. But I *will* persevere... I will *not* succumb...

Help meeeee...

16th July 2012
You *will* spend all your time with meeee...

I'm off out for a friends leaving do, Annie has just arrived, H is on the computer.

I tell Annie that a friend is picking me up at 7.15pm.

A minute or so later H says "Mummy sleep for 16 minutes!"

Oh no, I haven't got changed yet... I look at the computer and sure enough the time is 18.59. That little monkey is determined to make me lie down in bed with him and repeat all his rituals... no... I haven't got time!!!

Me: "Mummy sleep for ONE minute..."

H: "Clock!" (He means the kitchen timer I can't find!)

Me: "No clock today, Mummy count 60 seconds. 60 seconds is one minute."

We are now in my bed.

"1... 2... 3..."

"Mummy's arms is under!"

"Mummy's arms is under... 4... 5... 6..."

"Mummy neck is under."

"Mummy neck is under... 7... 8... 9..."

"H arms is under..."

Well you get the picture.

Eventually I am given permission to get out of bed. I've just got time to sling a new top on – no time to change my jeans, never mind – and grab my bag and the card and present I've got for my friend. Haven't got time to wrap it now... never mind... she knows me well enough... an old carrier bag will have to do! I'm off out!

Could really do with that holiday now...!

Chapter 9 Appendix

Holidays!!

Deep breath... and relax!!

Yes I know it's an appendix – holidays like this are a rare slice of respite for all the family: maybe not enough for a whole chapter, but I feel it deserves its own little section!

21st July 2012
St Ouen's beach, Jersey

We are staying with our lovely family again in the Channel Islands so they can be an extra pair of hands for us.

A great start to our holiday, a 5 mile beach, so sparsely populated that H can throw sand into the water to his heart's content and jump over the little waves, while G tows Steve up and down the vast shoreline.
I know they can be bloody difficult sometimes; but these lovely moments of child-like joy from our boys just being children on a vast expanse of beach are made all the more precious for that.

I actually felt so happy at one point I could have cried...
Truly wonderful to see.

21st July 2012
Waitrose on Jersey (the milk's labelled differently you know!)

Well generally it's good to have the other half around... except for the time we were busy bickering over which milk to get!
"This one's only 1% fat... yes but that's the same as skimmed and I don't like it... get the green one..."
After a minute or so of this I twigged that H was getting quite agitated... cue slamming down on knees / screaming session.
Oh dear.

2 days later...
"Mummy and Daddy weren't cross Waitrose...?"
"Yes that's right..."
Sigh.

I blame the husband!!

(Love him really!)

24th July 2012
Memory

"Play place September!" (He means a soft play place we last went to about 3 years ago.)
Me: "No Play place... Playbarn in September." (This is now our soft play place of choice!)
"H push little boy September Playbarn!!"

Please, no!

25th July 2012
Stroke ice cream

H:"Ice cream van, soft ice cream... stroke ice cream..."
 Ok it's soft, we stroke things softly...
"Fall over ice cream..." Eh? What?!

25th July 2012
Scary butterflies...

Grosnez castle, Jersey. We are among a stunning backdrop of romantic castle ruins on rocky cliffs; smothered with a blanket of tri-coloured heather sprinkled with bright yellow vetch...
Next time remind me not to take the autistic child I now know is petrified of butterflies...

Cue H launching himself into my arms every 30 seconds and me staggering down rocky pathways with him in my arms.
H is keeping up a mantra of: "Butterfly won't hurt... it's ok butterfly... butterfly is...?" looking around frantically at the masses of insects flittering about.
Ouch, my back.

We love going to stay with our family on Jersey; all of us. As well as helping us here and there every evening they always try to have the boys for a whole day so we can go out.
I used to love walking along cliff paths before we could no longer do it with the boys and buggies. It's something Steve and I shared. On our "day off" this year we parked up at Groznez (where the scary butterflies were) and walked along to Plemont beach. The path was slightly overgrown, so we were walking through periods of hush among the brambles and gorse, then coming out to little pockets of distant waves crashing against the cliffs. Such a peaceful place.
At Plemont there is a big stairway down the rocky cliffs to the beach: unfortunately it was high tide! Really should've checked that before we set out, oh well! Had lunch in the cafe, then sat right down the end of the steps by the crashing waves; me with my book, Steve with his camera. Both of us giggling at the tourists who were determined to stand right behind the biggest rock, getting soaked by the waves for their pains. Slightly worried watching the crazy local kids who were jumping from the rocks into the sea that swirled around back into the caves.
A lovely day together; a little taste of the few days we are yet to have when the boys go to the "SSAFA holiday house."

4th – 9th August 2012
Second honeymoon!!

Well that SSAFA holiday for the kids I was telling you about? We've dropped them off at the special centre. It's a wonderful place: a great big barn conversion set out around a courtyard, one to one helpers for all the children, as well as nursing staff and night sitters to stay up for those nocturnal lads and lasses.

After a prolonged chat with the staff and the volunteers who will be looking after our boys we say goodbye (for a whole 5 nights!!) and drive off up to Steve's work where we will stay in his room. I've never seen the area he has called home for over 2 years so I'm really looking forward to it. We are booked in that evening for a pub meal with 2 other couples who are also there, our paths have all crossed before. One of the couples I haven't seen for over 8 years: they used to be our neighbours on another base.

We get back to Steve's room, I'm really quite giddy. Those sleeping tablets I spoke about are stashed safely in my bag, I'm determined to get some quality kip!

Well the next few days are amazing, we re-discover things we used to like doing together. Ok steady... there's no need to get smutty!!

Exploring different historical old towns.

Going into all the most cluttered nick-nacky shops just because we can, no buggies or grabbing hands!

Visiting an open air museum and actually taking time to read boards and see everything.

Having a leisurely cream tea at an old castle.

Just being together, not having to worry about anyone but ourselves; and yes, I know how selfish that sounds.

It was a really special time to have away from our lads, but it was fabulous to have them back too. I got as many "stealth hugs" from G as I could get: hugging him around the waist whilst keeping my head down at that level so it's not too much for him. And H loves "squeeeeezy hugs!" Wrapping my arms around him and squeezing as tight as I can whilst we say "squeeeeeze!!" together.

When we went to pick up the boys they had had a fantastic time. I was driving out of the gate when H started asking me: "SSAFA holiday house in December...?"

Nice try! He knows when all the school holidays are you see...
We're so lucky that we were able to make use of this facility while Steve is in the RAF. I wish all my friends that struggle could access something like this...

Well folks, we are back home from our holidays again, let normal service resume!

Chapter 10

I don't want to jinx it but...

Deep breath... and relax!!

We are back home from our holidays again, let normal service resume!

17th August 2012
SO inappropriate

I'm knackered, just flomped on the sofa with my feet up for a few minutes. I'm trying to sort my brain for the next step in preparing to move house, Annie is packing a few bits in the lounge with us. H is sat on the sofa by my feet when he suddenly flops forward and headbutts my crotch with some force.
Me: "Aaarrgh...!!" (I couldn't help it, it hurt ok?!)
H: "Hurt private?"
I hear Annie hastily decamp to the kitchen – she knows what's coming.
"Sticker on private... sticker off private..."
I am having to put my hand on my bits to simulate a plaster being put on and off. I can hear Annie chortling away in the kitchen whilst I try not to be overcome by hysteria.

"Kiss it better private."

I hear a hastily smothered shout from the kitchen.

That's it, I'm now crying with laughter, having to repeat this after H several times as my voice now sounds wrong to him, simultaneously patting my groin whilst making a kissing noise.

"Rub it better private..."

Oh please, no more...

19th August 2012
"Father Christmas mouth!"

H is in the bath playing with bubbles. He has made a little goatee beard.

"H Father Christmas mouth!!"

19th August 2012
"Together we are stronger"

Choir members were asked to write a piece about someone who has made them stronger or influenced them by the Military Wives Choir Foundation, as part of the promotion for the new album.

The following is the piece I wrote, but it seemed appropriate to be included in my diary as it was from the heart and does relate to our boys.

My hubby and I have been blessed with 2 very different lads, both severely affected by autism. One lad speaks, the other doesn't: they have massive communication issues, can have behavioural meltdowns and self-harm, and may be dependent on us for life. I won't lie, it's hard. Really hard.

Being a forces wife also has its own challenges, as well as fantastic rewards.

The RAF community have taken my boys to their heart, and have rallied behind us in very difficult times. I am very lucky to have made some good friends, and feel blessed to be part of the choir. So many people have touched my life: far too many to mention. I am so grateful to all these, friends and family, who have undoubtedly helped me stay sane and kept me strong!

But, ultimately, it's our 2 boys themselves who have made me who I am today. Needing to understand them, learning to communicate with them, has meant I have *had* to become strong.

Loving my complex, bewildering, funny, maddening and heartbreakingly delightful boys: this has made me stronger.

I know, I know, you can put the sick bags away now!

August – September 2012
Moving house

So much for the idea of buying a newish bungalow so we'd have no worries about stairs or maintenance.
Two autistic kids, we moved into a 200 year old house before it was ready. Doors are off their hinges, tools are everywhere, the stairs are incredibly steep and narrow. But guess what? The boys have settled in really well. Who knew?!

I had it all planned out: we would do any work that needed doing, change those wobbly banisters with the too wide spindles, have the dedicated 'sensory room' for G all ready before we moved in. Yes. Well.

We got the keys in mid-April. Had damp course done, new skirting boards, plastering, new roof... then a French drain put in, painting and decorating done, all thanks to friends and family. We finally took the plunge in August even though the banisters and sensory room weren't done... Oh well, school was starting soon and we needed to have at least a few days in the new place before we embarked on a different bus for G and a whole different school run for H.

The OT's were great in trying to help make the transition as smooth as possible; but bizarrely in the end it wasn't that awful!

There were a few issues to be addressed:
the actual move and the lead up to it

the clash in school drop off / pick up times
the hoped for change in the bedtime routine (Please, please let him stay in his own bed...)

The OT suggested that sometimes the big changes are easier to deal with than the small ones, so we were hoping that with H's bedtime rituals we could wipe the slate clean so to speak. Remember all that forced repeating of arms under, neck under, etc?!
As far as G went, I didn't really prepare him at all, as it's a little difficult to know just how he feels about this sort of thing. As long as G has adults around to play with he really doesn't seem to be worried. He always has lots of cuddles these days, and he is always reassured about the people in his life and when he will see them again.
H was the one I was worrying about.

So here's what we did:
Had a chart with "Today I will sleep at" and spaces for each day over 2 weeks where I could Velcro pictures of the relevant house: old home, respite home, new home.
We also had pictures stuck up by the doors saying the old home was finished, and Mummy, Daddy, G and H now lived at the new place; the new place was now home.
We got a folder with 6 pages to turn over:

- Time for bed
- Under the duvet
- Disk on
- Eyes closed
- Light off
- Stay in H's bedroom, wait for the bell

The bell was an alarm clock set for 7am or thereabouts. The idea being that H doesn't keep coming in to OUR bed!! (Please...!!?)

Here are the results:
H accepted the 'sleep' calendar really well. He did say about going home a few times, but then would parrot "...old home all empty... new house is now home."
We have really had no problems with this at all.

The bedtime folder went really well, he asked for "cat rug" but I just said "we don't have cat rug at new house!" and he seemed to accept it. The same with Big Pooh and Big Dog, I just said we don't have them at new house and because it was different he accepted it. Result! No more death by repeating!!

The only addition he made was after we had read through the pages on the folder, he said "Mummy can shut the door." That's fine by me!

Now *please* let him sleep through the night...

Damn!

Sadly the sleeping through the night thing wasn't to be. Bugger.

Each time he gets up in the night to come to me I direct him back to bed, we have to do the folder *again*...

Sadly by the 4th or 5th time he comes in I'm so exhausted I'm sleeping through it, kind of cancelling out all the other returns I've done... arrgh!

H did go through a phase where he obviously didn't get the concept of the alarm clock. The idea was it would go off outside his bedroom and that meant he could leave his room.

"Mummy get beep beep green clock!"

Damn, this isn't how it's supposed to work!

Unfortunately because I was comatose before it was time to get up and H had already snuck into my bed, we then needed the "green clock" to go off before we were allowed to get out of bed. (If I'd set the alarm clock for 5am that might have worked better, but let's face it that was *never* going to happen.)

I had to go get the green clock, get back into bed, make it beep manually, *then* we could get up.

Sigh.

Have discussed with the OT how persevering with returning H to bed is all very well, but until I get door exit alarms to wake me in the night every time, there's not a lot of point. I mean we're not exactly being consistent are we.

So the assistive living people are going to get me sensor alarms, some sort of voice activated thing where he can hear me saying "Time for bed!!" and maybe a monitor for us to see him when he's getting up even before we've gone to bed.

So when we get this stuff I can be springing up every hour in the night again – can't wait!!!

Well that's the plan anyway, watch this space!

As for the clash in school times, I'm afraid I'm having to pick up H 20 minutes early every day in order to be home in time for G's bus.

Never mind though, one thing at a time. I'm so happy the going to bed bit is easier now, as that was *really* getting me down.

14th September 2012 Making conversation

In the morning - H: "G have respiridone medicine."
A moment later: "G have respiridone medicine!!!"
Me: "Yes G is having respiridone medicine."
We finally get the meds in G.
"G have more respiridone medicine!" (Grinning.)
Me: "That's funny! G doesn't have more respiridone medicine!"
H: "G have respiridone medicine in the evening."
"Yes that's right, clever boy."

14th September 2012 Calmer times!

H has really relaxed things on the forced repeated echolalia front.
Now, going to school from the new house:
"Over the big river bridge... over the railway bridge, 2 bridges, under the bridge, another bridge..." (that's what happens when you live on the other side of the river!)
"Roundabout, traffic lights on the roundabout... street lights, lots of them street lights..."
Up to this point I can usually now say a variation of "Yes that's right, good boy H!" etc.
About 10 minutes in he starts getting a little agitated:
"Boats on the little river bridge?!?"
I'll have to repeat him, then we are back to "Yes that's right..."

15th September 2012 Applying logic

Parking by a garden area with a war memorial in town.
"I see the grass town!"

There is a circular bench in the pedestrian area in town.
"I see the people roundabout!"

I love the way H sees the world...

19th September 2012 Unprompted affection

I'm lying on the sofa in the lounge watching H playing intently on his ipod thinking how beautiful he is; wondering how it would have been for him a hundred years ago when this technology didn't exist.
After a few minutes H looks over at me and grins: "SO gorgeous!!"
I agree with him.
He comes over and gives me a cuddle.
Me: "I love you."
H: "SO much!! I love you *so* much!!!"

19th September 2012 Remembering things again

Last night G was coughing into Annie's face, H copied. He was then told not to do it.
Today we've got: "Coughing, spiky face... coughing hurt your face..."

22nd September 2012 Doctor H

H likes to direct us when medicating G, and can get stressed if there isn't a quick enough response.
Me talking in code to Steve: "Has G had you know what?"
H: "G have respiridone!!"

Don't know who I thought I was fooling really.

27th September 2012 Dancing together

Me and my G are dancing hand in hand along to "Madness" by Muse. Followed by a squeezy hug "pick up" whilst we sway to the music...

I think the professionals call this intensive interaction...

30th September 2012 Classical Brits preparation

I am packing and preparing for what is a massive event for me: singing live with the Military Wives choir at the Classical Brit Awards at the Royal Albert Hall. It is going to be televised at the weekend. This is immense... it is actually blowing my mind... breathe... breathe... "Mummy get log off."
Eh? What?!
"Mummy get log off!!"
Oh right, H wants me to turn the computer off for him after finishing his game. He comes for a cuddle:
"SO much!!" I tell him I love him so much, can't get enough of squeezing him... oh right, ok he's gone again.

Ok: packing, itinerary. Gareth Malone is conducting, Andrew Lloyd Webber and Gary Barlow will be accompanying us on pianos... eek... eek...
Ok better practice singing. Right, used to singing soprano on this song but have been drafted into the lower alto part... stick the backing track on...
"Sing it louder, sing it clearer, knowing everyone will hear you..." (yes, like millions of people when this is televised... breathe... breathe...)

In bounds G.
Grinning up into my face he grabs my hands and we start bouncing and dancing around the room. His head is thrown back, eyes half closed, laughing, laughing.

I love that boy so much I could burst with it... I'm trying to sing, can't breathe for dancing and laughing...

Thank you my lads for keeping it real!

6th October 2012 More logic

We are in Morrisons supermarket, there are coloured pictures high up on the windows.
H: "I see the church shop!"
Well I guess they are a little bit like stained glass windows.

Me: "There are coloured windows in the shop."
H: "I see the coloured windows in the Morrisons church shop!"

6th October 2012 Poo is spit!

"H need new nappy."
He's done a poo, and is holding his shirt up.
I tickle his exposed tummy.
H: "Tummy poo!"
"There's no poo on your tummy, poo is in the nappy. Tummy is clean."
"Tummy, poo, dirty, spit... poo in spit nappy!"

I'm not going to win this one...

A minute later I'm changing his nappy:

H: "Poo is spit!!"
Me, trying not to laugh: "Poo is poo!"
H: "Winnie the Pooh, spit, dirty, Winnie the Pooh dirty!!"
A minute later...
"Georgie porgie pudding and pie..."

Oh I do love that boy...

7th October 2012 Trying to communicate

H: "Red clock... Red clock at home..."
He leads me upstairs to the bathroom.
"Red like the H's clock at bathroom... at home..."
It's a foam clock that you can stick on the bathroom tiles.

He doesn't seem to want it, just to tell me he was thinking about it I guess.

10th October 2012
Naming things yourself

H: "Orange sound?"
This is a small orange button 'talking tin' that goes to and from G's school. It's stuck with velcro to a piece of card with the symbol for 'news' on it. This symbol has an open rosebud type mouth with a speech bubble coming from it. The upper lip drops to a bit of a point in the centre.

"G like a wobbly tooth talking news!!"
This is now H's name for that particular piece of card.
Ok I guess that upper lip could look like a gummy bit where a tooth has fallen out...?

"Cars going pyramid zebra crossing road."
This is actually just his name for a zebra crossing, I think we have a bit of an association with triangular warning signs.

I know, I know, it's turning into the H show, bear with me! G bless him is being so good at going with the flow at the moment... though I probably shouldn't say that out loud? I might jinx it again!

11th October 2012
I'm getting better... honest!

Just when I think I'm remembering all the rituals!

I know now that H cannot get into the car without having his school bag put on his back properly, complete with fastened chest straps. Doesn't matter if I've pulled up just outside the school and it takes around 10 seconds to get to the car, we need the bag on first before taking it off again to get in.

That's fine, we get back to the car, bag off, we both get into the car, H has his drink bottle which he puts into the cup holder...

H: "Bag on."

Me: "We don't have bag on in the car!"

H: "Car open, bag on."

Ok, not going to argue. Out I get, let H out, put the bag on...

"Drink in the bag."

Oh, right! I knew I'd forgotten something... I put the bottle into the netty pocket on the side of the rucksack, H craning his neck around to see.

"Bag off, drink in the car..."

I *am* getting better at understanding his autistic world...

After school: Ok I *thought* I was getting better...

I am trying to type a letter on the computer. H asks for hoop de loop saga game.

"Mummy's turn first then hoop de loop saga. H play with ipad in the arch room. (It has an arched doorway.) This is not an unusual request from me, and he is usually happy to comply these days...

5 minutes later H is screaming from the arch room:

"You want no!"

I quickly hustle in: "What's the matter H?"

"You want no, you want no, you want no, arrgh, you want no, ARRGH!"

I can't seem to calm him down here so I just walk away.

"Mummy in the arch room!"

I go back.

"You want yes... you want yes... Mummy in the arch room there..."

More screaming and throwing himself on the floor, scraping his wrists on the carpet.

We go through the calming ritual, I manage to get him on his ipad again and into his little tent.

I go back to typing my letter.

H comes out: "Hoop de loop saga."

"Mummy's turn first then hoop de loop saga."

"Hoop de loop saga!!"

Meltdown time again.

Obviously we are a little twitchy today and can't do the waiting thing right now.

I'm mentally slapping my head for being so stupid... even though on the surface he had initially seemed happy to wait, he had actually just wanted the game straight away...

12th October 2012
You got up too soon!!

Steve is home this week so he has the pleasure of sorting nocturnal H while I catch up on kip in a room downstairs.

I wake up at 8am, it's fine, Steve will be sorting G ready for his bus at 10 past.

I come out into an eerily quiet downstairs... there is a scuffling in the kitchen...

I find G happily wandering around on the kitchen worktops investigating the cupboards. In his sleepsuit, no sign of hubby.

I'm galvanised into action and yell up the stairs for Steve to come help dress G while I prepare his meds.

He tells me H was up half 4 to half 6 so had understandably slept in.

Hubby and I then both go downstairs to sort G.

A couple of minutes later I hear distant howling... "You want no, you want no, you want NO!!!"
Arrgh, we're back to that again!
"What's the matter H?"
After a few minutes he manages to tell me...
"Daddy there, Daddy in bed!!"

Oh right. It's been a little while since *I've* had to wait for permission to get out of bed in the morning, but now Daddy needs permission to get up too.

You see, I'll never stop having to learn...

13th October 2012
Freedom...

On very rare occasions, we manage to match up G going to the carer's with H going to his residential unit. We go off to town: shopping, cinema, pizza... well you've got to squeeze it all in haven't you! A night without the boys...

Steve and I have gone to town. No boys.
Steve has wandered off to do some bits while I spend an hour, yes an hour, in a bra shop choosing underwear. (Let's just say I'm not an average size so unfortunately grabbing something off the peg from a regular high street shop is not an option.)
After spending an obscene amount of money on 2 bras and some knickers I wander around the market. I'm bimbling about, taking ages to look at stuff, I've got that feeling you get: a bit like when you're used to carrying a heavy shoulder bag, and suddenly you're not holding anything. No buggies, no worries about escaping children, no bag of food and continence products to lug about.

A curious feeling: I'm listening to a busker, it's a brisk sunny day, I feel light inside. It takes a moment to recognise it: it's joy, the freedom!

16th October 2012
Normal for us

1am
G has taken himself into my bed, all I can see are an arm and a leg sticking out from under the duvet. As H will come in in the night it's quite tempting to leave G there and see if H will accept him as a worthy substitute for me in the bed... hmm... best not.

5am
I'm in my own bed, H is here now too – must have slept through that again - I can hear some squeaking... oh it's G. I go and get him something from the food cupboard then redirect him to the ball pool... back to bed, zzz...

5.50am
Ow!! Damn! Just got an elbow in the eye socket... tried not to yell too much but we are now doing the "sticker on, sticker off" ritual in bed, that's fine. We are kissing and rubbing better H's elbow though, not my eye! Oh well, never mind!

6.05am
H goes off to bring the ipad back to bed. After a few minutes G comes in again and H goes off downstairs. I'm a little tired... zzz...
"Arrgh!!"
Damn, it's H yelling from downstairs, he doesn't sound happy. He is stressing over a rocking "gaming" chair we were given as he is trying to hold the lighter top end to the ground.
H: "What's the matter H?"
Me: Ditto.
H: "Arrgh, arrgh!!"
Me, again: "What's the matter H?"
It's no good, he's gone beyond it now.
Slaps himself with both hands on his cheeks and flops backwards onto the floor.
H: "Hurt your chin!"
We are rubbing it better again and have a big squeezy cuddle.
We are ok again. It's quiet in the other room – too quiet. Where's G, I know I locked all the doors last night..? Oh there he is straddling

the sink having rifled through the cupboards. I lift him down, grabbing a stealth squeezy hug on the way!

He trots off jogging on his toes, twiddling a bit of ripped cloth. He's happy.

Enter H, still a little fragile: "Mummy sleep with H in G's bed."

Oh ok then let's go, budge up.

Not actually sleeping, you understand. We lie there while H plays on the iPad.

7am

"Mummy sleep with H in Mummy and Daddy's room."

Ok, we are getting nearer to full reset mode.

I get into bed, H cuddles me again: "H sad."

Me: "H sad? Oh dear." I hold him tight and rub his back.

He gets into bed next to me.

More iPad.

7.20am

Me: "I'm getting up now."

H: "Mummy can get up!"

Downstairs, H has a big smile: "Jelly egg sweet!"

Me: "We don't have sweets for breakfast!"

H grinning: "Jelly egg sweets dirty for breakfast!!"

And… the happy boy is back!

18th October 2012
Make up your own sentences – works for me

We are driving along.

H: "Cars going zebra pyramid crossing lights."

Me: "Yes, that's right."

I'm not even going to argue about it anymore. If it makes him happy, that's fine by me!

20th October 2012
It's shopping, but not as *you* know it...

We're in town, both boys are in buggies. Or as H says: "Walking around the shops and cafe town!"

I need a long sleeved black top for choir, so we go into a department store.

H: "Clothes shop, Mummy getting clothes!"

I know I'm on a bit of a time limit with H here so after looking for a minute unsuccessfully, I grab one of the shop assistants. I describe what I want and she wanders off to find some bits, me following with H.

"Mummy getting clothes!"

"Yes, Mummy is looking at clothes, look!" I hold up a cardigan, then try it on.

He's pacified and goes back to his ipod.

I try on a couple of different things. Steve says he'll go and look upstairs with G in the lift. H hears the word "lift" and gets excited so we have to swap boys, H going up with Steve.

I'm with the shop assistant looking at the in-store computer for fancy cardigans. I'm swivelling my head around every few seconds as G takes his shoes off, and tucks his knees up under him in preparation for escaping the buggy. The shop assistant is joining in with the G-watching so we are fine.

Later we swap boys again as G is getting ever more fidgety. Steve takes him off to the food hall in search of cheese twists.

The cardi I want to try is out of stock in my size, so while the very helpful shop assistant is noting down codes for me to look up the clothes online, H is now starting to yell: "Mummy get pay the lady!!"

In his world that's what happens: you go in a shop, then come out again after you pay someone. He's getting a bit frantic (and frankly, very loud) so sneaking up to the wrong end of the queue for the tills I collar a girl from the changing rooms.

"Can you do me a favour please? Just stand here by the end of the tills and pretend to take my money...?"

She looks a little bewildered but bears with me, I get H to say goodbye to her so he knows we're done, then make a hasty exit. I'm a little frazzled, so when I decide to look in another shop I decide to trade children with Steve again. I feel in the mood for some G-watching, rather than H-repeating/pacifying.

Things are ticking away nicely at home, usual stuff going on with the boys, but I've decided to take the plunge and cut G's hair this week. Will get the clippers out and Annie and me will just have to grit our teeth and pin him down. It's not so much rock star / beach bum hair now, it's more of a matted fur ball / birds nest style. Decision made; if I do it on a longer blade I still won't have to do it again for months, maybe not until next summer - yippee!!

21st October 2012
A&E...

So I've left hubby in charge of the boys as I am singing with the choir this morning. We finish warming up when I hear my phone go, and spy 3 missed calls from Steve. Whoops.
G has slipped over and gashed the back of his head. Steve is in the car on his way to me to hand over H before going to the hospital for possible stitches.
G is quite distressed and won't let me near his head to look but Steve says there is quite a gash so off they go. H is very good and sits with me in the church while I wait to do the song.

Steve meanwhile is up A&E with G. By now of course G has calmed down and is gleefully skipping around. It's good to know he cheered everyone up by bouncing up and down the length of the waiting room, then gave a guy palpitations when he twiddled the toes at the end of the plaster cast on his wife's busted leg! (Yes, G still has that foot fetish!) She found it quite funny though.
After an hour they go into the triage bit and wait another hour. G is fine all this time, quite happy. Sadly this stopped as soon as they tried to glue the gash on his head. It took 4 of them to hold him down. I'm quite glad I wasn't there to hear the screams, poor boy!
So. No swimming and no hair-washing for a week, and therefore I'm guessing, NO attacking your son with electric hair clippers.

Damn.

22nd October 2012
Can I stop flinching now?

H has had another little wobble in the car: he decided to take his shoes off then wanted instant help from me to put them back on. I think he put his own shoes on again after PE and got the tongues stuck inside, that's fair enough if it was uncomfortable. He waits until he's safely with me though, driving along the main road before asking for help – arrgh!

It's the requirement of the instant response that still has me a little twitchy. Amid the screaming and shouting I'm aware of the potential missile of the full drink bottle in his flailing hand. I keep saying I'll put his shoes on in the car at home, I'm hoping this will be enough to stop the kind of meltdown that makes him totally lose control of himself, and especially the hand holding that bottle.

I'm afraid I'm totally on tenterhooks, angling my head as far over to the right as possible, I figure if I can hide behind the headrest a little I'll be ok... no, still nowhere to pull over... damn...

Oh... I think it's ok, he has started to cry properly now and is asking for a cuddle... still have to put off the cuddle until we are home... "Cuddle hand!" Ok I can do that.

I reach around and ruffle his hair and wipe his wet cheeks. See? That was actually ok... maybe I can relax a little about this stuff...?

24th October 2012
Misunderstandings, insomnia and the anticipation of sleep...

1am

I'm still up, slightly buzzing from choir night, as well as slightly starving, so am making my way through a family pack size of crisps. Down comes H.

Up we go again, but he won't settle. He is muttering about something yogurt and a spoon.

"Amberdon yogurt!"

I tell him I'll get a yogurt but that's not it: "No yogurt... Yes yogurt... No there... Amberdon yogurt... spoon... amberdon spoon yogurt!!!"

???! He rather quickly melts down in his half asleep state, legs flailing the duvet off, grabbing my hand, alternately pushing me away, but at the same time not letting me go. I'm kind of trapped, he doesn't want comfort but wants something from me. Yet every time I go towards his bedroom door to try and fetch a yogurt and spoon (the closest things to what he seems to want) he screams even louder, if that's possible.

I'm tired too and fast getting frustrated, starting to say things like "What, H? I don't understand!" This is obviously not helpful.

I go down and get the yogurt and spoon. I've given up, it's all I can think of.

He is pretty much beside himself by the time I get back up, whacks himself multiple times on the head, then wanting the comforting routine of sticker on / off etc.

Oh good I think, we can re-set.

Well up to a point anyway!

He drags me downstairs, then for the next 10 minutes proceeds to tow me around the ground floor by my little finger. He has it in a vice-like grip, and to be honest it's not at an optimum angle. I wonder idly if the agony engendered by a broken digit would enable me to drive him to school in the morning before checking myself into the hospital for splinting. Getting both boys into the car at 2am to sort myself out wouldn't really be on my wish list of potential things to do.

Oh it's ok, he's easing off. After being dragged to the kitchen cupboards, the lounge, and rather inexplicably the wood burner I'm repeating over and over "Amberdon yogurt all gone, H have apricot yogurt!"

I was really hoping that he meant apricot yogurt, but it doesn't seem like it is. Oh well, he's knackered and it seems like he's finally going to go for it.

We do the yogurt, then up to bed, I manage to do his bedtime folder routine and get out of his room.

Damn, G meanwhile has woken up and put himself in my bed. Grrr...

I put him back into his own bed, and go to bed myself.

10 minutes later...
In comes G. He's having a squeaking bouncing session. Great, shove that earplug further in...

Later still...
H has come into my bed, G is on the other side... oh whatever...zzz

4am
H is awake, I think G has moved himself from my bed and curled up in a duvet on the floor...
H: "Ipad!"
Oh God. Now?!
Me: "H get ipad from the arch room."
Off he goes. At least he can do that himself now, thank goodness. I feel grim from lack of sleep and I'm finding it difficult to surface.
H is back in bed with the ipad making it's musical squeaks and bangs. Sleep.

6am
I come to and see H lying next to me asleep with the ipad on his chest.
Time to close eyes again then.

7.30am
I'm up, H is awake, chilling with the ipad again. I've had to lug G to the top of the stairs to wake him up to get ready for school.
I stick a message on facebook asking Annie about H's "amberdon yogurt" request. I get a message back.
Apparently H had seen a pot of Ambrosia Devon custard last night and had been obsessing about it. She had given him half the pot.
Amberdon. Ambrosia.
Oh.

Later, after school...
Damn, just couldn't keep G in, and he is wandering in the garden in the rain in his sleepsuit.
Best get him in a hot bath then. At least he doesn't like his hair washed, a real plus when I've got to keep the glue on his wounded scalp dry.

Right, in the bath, oh that hair is so long and matted. Hmm, while he's in the bath might be able to cut his hair a bit... right, off to find some scissors.

Bugger, while I've gone I forgot about the hideously expensive scented candle! He has gouged a bit out and his chest and face is now rather red from whatever pungent oil was in there. Quick, wash it off...
Right, let's get snipping.

Good thing G isn't fussy about his coiffure... at least I *hope* he's not...

24th October 2012
Simple pleasures

Knackered again after last night, and Annie's coming this evening. I am already planning with happy anticipation what to cook myself for dinner, which I will then take into a hot bubble bath complete with trashy novel and a wood wick crackly candle...
Ahh... bliss...

I actually put something like this on my facebook status, tagging Annie so it would give her the 'heads up' on what I was doing when she got here.
Unfortunately it read like I was going in a hot bubble bath with her, which we all had a good laugh over. I really was in that semi punch-drunk state where you're so tired you're not quite with it. Trouble is flappy ears H then starts on about "Mummy bath with Marianne..."
Oh dear...
"No H, Mummy was talking about bath with Marianne."
H: "Mummy talking about bath with Marianne!"
Hmm... not sure that's any better! Good thing Annie knows what I'm like when I'm knackered!

24th October 2012
Parenting skills

I would just like to point out that any requests from H for "gin" are purely down to his new found love of wine gums. Sweets and reading: they are right up his street.

Nothing else.
Honest.

Maudlin ramble alert!

I'm not good at paperwork, filing, admin.
I'm currently Branch Officer of the local branch of the National Autistic Society. There is a very small core of committee members who keep things ticking over. We have raised funds which we use to finance all of the activities for our families. This is an important source of respite for a lot of families.

So I'm not good at it. But we need a Branch Officer, and no-one else is able to do it right now.

One of my biggest failings, however, is that I'm too hard on myself when I feel I've let someone down. I'm much tougher on myself than I would be on anyone else in the same situation, which is silly, I know.
I felt I should've known that a good friend of mine would be feeling low with everything that's happened to her recently; I should have contacted her sooner. Not a very good friend on my part, I felt: bad girl!! Though we got together and that was all fine, it was the beginning of the slide into a massive downer for me. Yep folks, when you're generally working on little sleep and elevated stress levels you can end up making a bit of an arse of yourself... I mean, I don't suppose she was sitting there thinking "that woman's a bit of a twat, how dare she not know I was struggling?" But I guess I have self-imposed standards that I aspire to, it wasn't what she may have thought of me that was the issue: it was the fact I hadn't tried to help her sooner when I could've done.

I then made a few other honest mistakes... A few of us were meeting up. I ended up leaving another friend high and dry on her tod at a tea room because I'd changed the venue and didn't tell her - I genuinely didn't think she was coming!!

Then I sent out emails to all the NAS members inviting them to a support group which wasn't actually on as it was a committee meeting, and had to hastily email a retraction – for goodness sake!

But when a friend sent me a message reassuring me that I wasn't actually doing a really crap job (I know, she was being kind!) it just tipped me over the edge. I mean really, if someone's having a bit of a difficult time, golden rule number 1 is never, ever, be nice!!!

Well that was it, made rather a tit of myself by then bawling my eyes out at the afore-mentioned meeting.

Oops!

At this point I just felt disgusted with myself for cocking everything up, and neglecting the NAS, because frankly I've been very happy being involved in the choir. It's been a bit of normal life, and I felt guilty about that, taking respite for myself through singing to the detriment of the NAS branch.

Honestly I wouldn't vilify anyone for the same behaviour for a second, but you do it to yourself, don't you. So I've been feeling rather emotional, stupidly, but I'll get over it!

Jeez, enough already!! See the big stick I beat myself with?! Just eat some damn chocolate and move on!!

Really, sometimes I think I've got a surfeit of empathy. Probably one of my greatest strengths, as well as one of my greatest weaknesses! People I care about, I worry about probably more than they want or need.

It used to be mooted that people on the autistic spectrum didn't have empathy – nonsense! In fact maybe it's just the opposite sometimes, I don't know.

Maybe that's my little foothold on the spectrum, I don't know. I never could meet my Mum's eyes very well when I was younger; I was aware of it before I knew anything about autism! I found it way too intense. Weird really. Hey ho. They say everyone's a little bit autistic don't they? Well that's just fine by me!

26th October 2012
Magic moments

It's strange how you can delight in squ-eeeezing the boy with his eyes blissfully closed, big smile on his face. Despite the fact that 5 minutes ago he had stripped and wiped his bum on the new chair... and his sleepsuit is now permeated with the smell of poo.

I swear these kids have magic powers...

27th October 2012
Changing the rules...

Waitrose.

Hubby has one of those gadgets that lets you scan your own shopping as you go round, so at the checkout they just scan the gadget and you pay.

We get to the tills, there are no signs to say you must take the gadget to a particular checkout. We are waiting nicely for our turn.

H: "Going to pay the man."

Me: "Yes, we are waiting to pay the man."

We get to the man.

Apparently we need to go to the customer services desk. There were no signs to say so... hmm.

Steve goes striding off with G, I attempt to follow.

"Pay the man!!!"

Oh God.

Full on screaming, arms thrashing (thank goodness I've got him in one of those special disabled child trollies) and general distress.

I go back to the till where "the man" is just leaving to go on his break.

I persuade him to go back, and talk to us so I can pretend to pay him. (Yes I have to do this a lot in shops.)

Thankfully he's game and agrees, I get H to say goodbye to the man, hopefully that will be it.

No. More screaming as I am trying to get him out of the shop.

"There!!!"

The screams are truly blood-curdling now. Everyone queuing at the till is staring.

He is banging his wrists against the wall, the door frame, the thing that you put the charity tokens in that they give out at the till...

Oh lord, the penny drops.

Because we didn't go through the till properly we didn't get a token...

Some people may think: "Oh for goodness sake boy what are you so upset about?!"

I'm ashamed to say maybe this would have been me at one time... now all I can think is: "Ruddy shop... why can't you put proper signs up at the tills to direct people *before* they start queuing?!"

All this was so avoidable... sigh...

31st October 2012
Welcome home...

I've been out for the night with choir again. Annie has once again stayed with H for the night while G has a night at his carers. I'm back late so H is already in bed on the second night.

1.30am

It's been a crazy couple of days, going off to London again with some of my choir buddies, I'm finding it difficult to wind down as it has been a bit of an emotional rollercoaster lately. I'm in bed doing some puzzles to try and switch off.

I hear H get up so head him off in the hallway. He squints at me and says "Marianne gone."

Me: "Yes that's right, Marianne gone. Mummy's here."

H, going back to his bed: "Hello Mummy."

After breakfast I am shattered, as I've been awake since before 6am, not good.

Later on we go to fetch G from the carers.

He is smiling into my face, hugging me, gripping me.

Welcome home.

1st November 2012
Tadpole boy

Took the boys swimming today with Annie's help, G's twice weekly sessions at school have really paid off! His little legs were paddling away, going sideways up and down the pool with his armbands on and a big smile on his face!

I thought half term was going to be difficult, but Annie thank goodness was there to help me out, hence the lovely swimming trip!

The thing is the nursery where the boys have been going to for years no longer felt able to accept G at the holiday club.
In the summer holidays they did tell me he had gouged the hand of one of the assistants and pulled her hair. Naturally I had apologised on his behalf; it seemed that he was getting frustrated, I had forgotten to take his buggy in that day which is a calming place for him, as he likes to be wheeled around outside. Never mind, it was all sorted out, or so I thought!

The first time I realised there was a problem was when I went to book him in for half term sessions. I've really relied on these in the past as a source of respite. It's not easy to find mainstream holiday activities where the boys are looked after so well, so it was a real blow to me to be told that because of that "incident" they didn't feel able to have G in that setting any more without additional help. Sadly no help was forthcoming. The nursery manager asked if I could approach the Forces charity SSAFA about the possibility of a volunteer helping, but that was just totally impractical as most of the volunteers were full time members of the forces themselves.

So Annie, bless her, clocked up loads of extra hours, which I had to owe her, as we went well over my monthly allowance. I really am so lucky to find such a dedicated personal assistant, what would we do without people like this?

Chapter 11

Damn. Jinxed it.

Choir for me is still going strong. That bunch of girls help me out more than they know just by letting me sing with them, more than that they are my friends.

We were on telly again the other day, promoting the album.

Another overnight stay in a hotel, I arranged for G to go to his carers, and for Annie to stay at our place with H.

It was great, I'm on a bit of an emotional rollercoaster at the moment though after the combined high of singing, spending child-free time with friends and being spoilt by staying in a hotel with unlimited breakfast. (Yum… how brilliant is this?!) I was quite lonely on my own again at home after the boys went to bed. It was all too easy to get on a bit of a downer, as my sleep is also getting worse and worse.

I've been awake at 1.30am minimum every night now for at least a week. I've now got some herbal tablets to try as I'm still between doctors since moving house and don't have any sleeping tablets left. Will see how the herbal tablets go. Failing that will try a snifter of port!

I do seem to be a bit up and down emotionally lately, I'm quite aware that I am 45 now: is it too soon to be menopausal?! Oh God, there's something to look forward to!

5th November 2012
Who is actually the "disabled" one?!

I have now started a blog on Facebook, as friends kept suggesting I should. So that's it, I've put myself out there. (A bit like this book really, except you lot can't comment back so easily!)

Intro to my blog:
"I've been writing for some time about life with my two gorgeous, crazy, infuriating and craftily intelligent boys, who also happen to have autism. Here are my attempts to be a good mother to two severely autistic boys whilst hampered by a neurotypical brain. Some people might call me the "normal" one: I call myself the one trying to understand two children fluent in another language while I'm still in the pidgin stages."

Well that kind of sums it up really.

9th November 2012
Awkward morning

5.20am
Am woken by a lot of squeaking amid the landing light going on. G is up then.
I took a sleeping tablet as well last night so am still really tired, damn. I nip to the loo where G tails me and pounces on the loo roll; oh well. I lock up the bathroom and crash back onto the mattress. 10 minutes later H comes in; he does kind of settle down so that's ok. G is quietly humming away, amusing himself.

6.30am
H is getting increasingly wriggly, I'm still *so* tired.
"Radio on..." and lots of repeating of "Mummy having a sleep!" (Clearly I'm not.)
G comes back into the bed with us, snuggling down by my feet.
"H sitting G!!"
Uh oh! This usually means he is sitting on G, hopefully just on his back rather than on his head – don't laugh, it does happen!

Me, hastily: "Downstairs!!"

8am

G's bus arrives.

He is more than ready for the off as he has been climbing and opening all the kitchen cupboard doors where he *thinks* I hide the back door key...he's not sussed the hiding place yet, hahaha!!

8.30am

I'm ready to set off for school with H. He grabs one of Steve's big jumpers and puts it over his head so he looks like a little brown ghost.

"H... Daddy... having a sleep, Daddy..."

He waddles out to the car like this and keeps it over him all the way to school.

My heart melts a little as I look at him, I guess he's missing Daddy...

9th November 2012
Saint G

G made some pizzas with olives on at school which have been sent home, so the boys are having them for tea. Well H eats his minus the olives, and G makes a lacy pattern in his by scraping his gnashers over the cheese topping.

Minutes later I find both boys on the floor, it looks like H is administering emergency dental treatment. G is kneeling on the floor, practically at Olympic limbo level as H crouches behind, one arm around G's neck. His free hand is dragging G's lips open into a horrific grimace.

Oh right, he's trying to feed G olives.

After the predicted tantrum from H after I've prised him off, saying "don't hurt G" all is calm again. Oh now he has hold of G's arm. They are stood together while H makes G slap his own head. Hold on, now he is marching G in and out of the room at speed, iPad in one hand, a handful of G's sleepsuit bunched in his other fist. They stop, and G happily bounces on the spot face to face with H.

When on earth did G get so laid back?!

9th November 2012
Hide and seek, fun and games

Great! G skipped off with the car key while H had a death grip around my neck whilst in one of his frets. Now I'm playing hunt the key, not easy as this is a big old house. Oh and I'm seriously sleep-deprived after a busy week so the tidy-up fairy hasn't come and the house looks like a shit pit. (Excuse the potty mouth.)
I'm laying bets it's in G's bed.
Any takers? No?!

Oh boy, the boys were trailing me around the house while I was searching for the key, when H got in a tussle at the top of the stairs with G. Naturally after I made them both safe H proceeded to speed up and down the dining room leaping onto his knee caps. He soon started screaming "cuddle" at me to repeat, which I obviously wasn't doing right as he got more and more irate about it. (And yes, I *was* actually cuddling him!) Cue another mother of the year moment as I snapped and yelled "CUDDLE!!" at the top of my lungs about 5 times.
Hmm... throat is quite sore now.
I think I need a drink.
Might have an ancient bottle of port somewhere...

10th November 2012
Think yourself thin...?

So you know when your lad comes into your bedroom at 3.30am asking you to open a bag of chocolate clusters and a bag of pears, and then you hide them behind your pillow so he doesn't eat the lot? Guess which I decided to gum my way through when I was half asleep and too knackered to get up? I swear, inside is a svelte, slinky sex bomb waiting to get out: I blame the kids!

Now where's the rest of that chocolate...?

11th November 2012
Lightning legs

Acceptance by the public

I've been very lucky so far, my boys being 8 and 11, that I've never been yelled at for their behaviour, or really vilified because of it. I've had the stony looks (understandable when your precious child has been hit by H Bomb) and the unwillingness to understand, if you like.
But on the whole, I've met some really lovely people who do totally accept it.
I do apologise, not for my boys themselves, as I do try to explain why they have done something: rather, I am apologising for my inability to control the situation.
I do try to explain particularly to children that my boys may not understand how to play "correctly" with them, and may push and shove them as their social awareness is very different. But that is my fault, if I have not been right on hand to stop that, that's my responsibility.

We are at the playbarn again, I have a friend helping me as Steve is away. I have warned her to be on the lookout. H needs to be constantly told to "play nicely" and "watch out for children on the big slide", as he can sometimes be a little heavy handed when he tries to join in play. G needs to be watched like a hawk around the tables, as he minesweeps for drink bottles, pastry and icing off cakes.

All seems fine, my friend is keeping a close tail on G, I'm sitting at the table with H while he scoffs chips. My friend who works there has just been into the party room with a birthday cake. A beautiful, pink and white iced, horse's head for a little girl's party. My friend comes back from the party room bearing the cake to be divided up amongst the children, biting her lip. In fact she is struggling to keep the smirk off her face.
She shows me the cake.
Minus a huge chunk of nose.
Oh lord.
I am mortified, worrying about the little girl's upset... but as my friend goes back into the kitchen to cut it up I can see the state of hysteria among the staff through a crack in the door... I am chortling and snorting away with my hand clamped over my mouth... oh dear...

Despite our shared hysterics and my seeming lack of care I felt bad and insisted on apologising to the parents. They were just brilliant. So understanding, they were asking about G, said not to worry their little girl hadn't even noticed the nose-less horse!

Later that evening: lightning legs strike 2...

Once again "lightning legs" thought it hilarious to streak upstairs and use my duvet as rather comfy loo roll.
Unfortunately I hadn't quite got round to putting the new cover on... oops, Queen of Housework I ain't...
Am now pricing up the difference between a new duvet, and industrial quantities of vanish cleaner.

I'm edging toward the new duvet...

12th October 2012
G vocalising

Kneeling on my lap, after asking for kisses: "Oof, oof... oof, oof..."
Later, stood in front of me, getting me to stand up: "Oh oh... oh, oh..."

I wish I knew what that meant... I know what I want it to mean...

13th October 2012
Well it *was* cold...

The first time H touched my boobs 2 or 3 years back, he was learning body parts, and labelled my chest "tummy." I told him it was not tummy, it was chest, but I'm afraid H then actually called that area "Not Tummy", soon shortened back down to "Tummy."

H and me are at the front door, I'm just getting the keys out of the cabinet.
Woah... what the...?!?

H, squeezing my nipple really quite hard through my top: "Mummy's tummy!"

Me: "H, don't touch Mummy's tummy!!"

That's fine, except he then proceeds to say "Tummy" over and over, whilst trying to grab me again.

Me: "Yes it's my tummy, ok..."

H: *"Don't touch Mummy's tummy!!"*

Oh right, he wanted me to repeat that. That's ok.

I'm quite glad he doesn't know the words nipple, boobs, breasts etc; tummy doesn't sound quite so inappropriate when he's talking about touching it!

14th October 2012
What is the real cause here...?

We have all come downstairs for breakfast. Daddy didn't come home last weekend as usual, so H asks if Daddy is coming to play next Friday. I tell him no Daddy on Friday, Daddy on Monday, which he repeats and seems happy with.

Later.

I'm getting G's school bits ready in the hallway for when his bus comes. H has left his breakfast on the table and is stood in the lounge whimpering. My attempts to find out what's wrong result in a full-blown   paddy:

"No what's the matter... there... there!!" (directing me back out to the hallway.)

O...   kay...

15 minutes of screaming, hand banging and wrist scraping follow.

H: "You want fire on your wrist!" I guess that's what it feels like to him after giving himself a carpet burn.

He finally lets me calm him down and goes back out to his breakfast.

"Mummy tidy up banana..." (take it away!) followed by "Banana on the table." (bring it back!)

He seems a little unsure of the banana so I stick a bit in his mouth. Just when I'm worrying if he is getting all sensory about picking up the banana...

"Mummy get orange."

Bless him. Must book myself in for crystal ball lessons!

Later still, G has gone to school on his bus.

H is at the table finishing off his cereal bar. I tell him I'm going to put clothes on. This is our normal routine, he repeats back to me which I then repeat back to him one more time.
Like I say, all normal.
I'm upstairs, all dressed when I hear distant shouting: "Mummy get downstairs!!"
Down I go... "It's ok H, I'm here."
"Mummy getting clothes on!"
Yes, I've got clothes on.
"Mummy get clothes on, Mummy and Daddy's bedroom!!"
Trying to explain I'm already dressed is not helping, so I disappear upstairs, come down again and tell him I have clothes on.
No, he's not playing.
He is screaming at me to take my clothes off, which I actually start to do in desperation... we are really late for school now and I've already left a phone message...
"Mummy clothes off Mummy and Daddy's bedroom!!!"
Right, now I'm not playing any more.
Cue more bashing and kicking at me from H, plus:
"Glasses fall off, oh dear!"
I hastily take my glasses off – these are my good ones, can't afford to have any more broken!
He gives me a death-squeeze cuddle, arms around my neck, chin digging in to my shoulder as hard as he can. Ow.
I finally manage to get him out to the car where he continues crying interspersed with yells most of the way to school, wanting his ipod game.

So what was it? Daddy not coming? The banana? Both... plus something else!?

15th November 2012
School run

The trouble with having two special needs children in two different schools when only one of them is eligible for the bus... and you have no-one else at home to wait for the one that is eligible, is that sooner or later there's going to be a glitch with the timings.

Cue MASSIVE gridlock on the main route. I've just done a fair impression of a rally driver through fenland villages, practically airborne as I'm yamming the car up and down through the gears on the lumpily tarmacked rollercoaster style roads as I attempt to get home in time.

Could do with a stiff drink now as my shoulders were hunched with tension in a wrestling pose throughout our road trip. Oh well, home alone with the boys so will have to make do with a hot cuppa!

Roll on husband being home full time...

15th November 2012
The impact of choir...

There was a time, up to about a year ago, when I was not allowed to sing along to the radio. Any attempt to do so would prompt a "hello?!?" from H. If I continued I would get an increasingly stressed: "Hello...? HELLO...?!?"
I don't get that any more, in fact I'm in trouble if I don't "sing at radio" – sometimes I have to make the words up if I don't know the song. Eleven months of going to choir and the following is what I now get.

Just now in the car, the boy band One Direction was playing. (No really - this is our Musical Director's favourite group!)
H: "Mummy singing."
Well I wasn't but here goes: lalalala let's go crazy, crazy...
"MUMMY SINGING!!"
Let's go cra...
"Mummy singing louder!!!"
LET'S GO CRAZY... oh, hold on a minute...

Sing it louder, sing it clearer... ("Sing!" The Military Wives song)
Smiling again: "Mummy singing at church!"

We rehearse in the church, in case you were wondering!

17th November 2012
One night...

Ok I know that H's autistic traits become a little more pronounced when he is anxious. By this point Daddy hadn't been home for 2 weeks, G didn't go to the carer's house last weekend like he should've done and Daddy hadn't come this Friday night for the weekend either.
Sadly these were things I couldn't do anything about. But I'm sure the following has at least a little to do with this.

12.45 am
Back from a great night out singing with the choir. I have a quick debrief with Annie before she leaves then grab a bite to eat – I'm starving!

1.20 am
H comes down just as I'm preparing to go up. He quickly whizzes under my duvet but I guide him back to his room with no problem; but then the hassle starts.

The next hour is then spent doing the following:
Doing the bedtime folder around 8 times interspersed with H saying lots of random stuff that seems to need telepathy to resolve.
"There...? There!! Light on... aho, aho, ahoo (wanting me to copy his pretend coughing noises) no aho, ahoo (not wanting me to copy him) yes aho, ahoo..." (I don't know any more what he wants!!)

"Lovely smile with Mummy, Mummy get camera!" Oh good grief anything for a quiet life! I get the camera and take a few pictures as he keeps asking for "smile with the camera."

Oh no, not this again, he's desperately trying to revert to one of the bedtime rituals he had at the old house: "Mummy get H close your eyes" which means me running my hand over his face to shut his eyes. This reminds me disturbingly of what they do to dead bodies in films...

I refuse as I don't want these rituals to creep in again: cue lots of screeching, crying, hitting of self and death-grip cuddles whilst pulling my hair.

I then have to spend a period lying in bed next to him, but unfortunately he kicks off again.

Bedtime folder again (groan...): "Mummy can shut the door... no..."

I end up doing "Mummy can shut the door" another 6 times.

"Mummy get H close your eyes!"

You know what? Sod it. I'll do whatever you want!!

2.30 am

Fan-bloody-tastic!! I'm finally getting into my own bed when I hear a big sigh from the dressing room area. Damn, G must've put himself to bed in there earlier... now the squeaking and humming is starting... bugger, bugger!!

G thinks it's breakfast time...

Oh well sleep is highly overrated...

3.30 am

I'm drifting in and out of micro kips as G is rambling around my room squeaking... I can still hear H chatting to himself in his room.

4.30 am

H comes in to me again... he asks me if he can get ipad... fine, whatever... I don't think I could move right now if the house was on fire...zzz

6.30am

H had sparked out earlier but G is squeaking again so I guess it's wake up time.

I soon see the trail of destruction G has left in his wake as I go downstairs.

So all-in-all a fantastic late night out singing with my choir buddies was followed by an all-nighter pulled by my tag-teaming boys - that's karma I guess!

The place now looks like a team of sniffer dogs has been through it: empty packets, chunks of half-chewed malt loaf and a snow storm of shredded sanitary towels. I did think the kids might be running feral by Monday as it's just the 3 of us; I'm running on fumes and G has been awake since half 2 with no signs of stopping.

But I'm feeling almost alive after finding half a leftover pack of white chocolate buttons...

17th November 2012
A helping hand

After last night I'm about as knackered as I've ever been. I'm pottering on the computer while the boys have breakfast and put a note about it on my blog. Suddenly I get texts and messages offering help. In fact I'm so very tired I'm almost in tears over people's kindness!

One of my choir friends comes over via KFC. After some spicy chicken wings I'm feeling almost human again, so decide to get out with the boys while the going's good. We go on the ferry across the river to town. G likes the boat so much that he won't get off. While I'm struggling with the buggies and H up the long flight of steps, my friend manages to manhandle G off the boat. The driver soon takes pity on her and I see him lugging G up the steps.

He is rather heavy - I'm pretty sure the next time the boatman sees us coming the ferry will be leaving early!

18th November 2012
Entertaining the kids

Right, it's sunny. I'm feeling tired but need to get the boys out somewhere before my body gives up for the day!

Some choir friends go to church: I don't, but will shamelessly abuse the after service tea so I can have adult interaction for half an hour and the boys can see some other face than mine!

Right, off to Waitrose for a bit of Sunday shopping... G is on his reins and H is in the disabled child's trolley that actually has a working seatbelt. This shop we can do as the aisles are wide enough and empty enough for me to stop G helping himself to whatever takes his fancy. Having said that it's a given that G is going to have his lunch going around the shop. As a treat I open a pack of cheese sandwich biscuits – he only eats the middle cheesy bit. Must remember to chuck the de-cheesed biscuits out of my handbag this time...

Well I've spent £95 for an hour and a half's time in here; rather more expensive than the play barn but much less stressful – and I've got 20 quid's worth of booze to assist in the sleeping process later...

21st November 2012
Training for sleep deprivation

Steve is due to finish his time in the RAF soon so will be home for good. Once he's here full time I will be activating "Project Get your arse back in bed right NOW Mummy is VERY TIRED!!!" ... ermm... I mean "Project Bedtime." After all, I know Hubby will want to be involved with endlessly getting up in the night...!! Just haven't told him yet...

So: this thing where H has been coming into our bed every night for 5 years.

As I am pretty comatose after 4am I have now got gadgets from the helpful Assistive Living people to enable me to wake up when H comes out of his room so I can keep putting him back.

I thought it should probably involve some sort of electrified cattle prod contraption to get me up, a la Wallace and Gromit, but no, it's just a series of door sensors rigged up to a bleeper.

As of today, I am going to attempt to descend back into the daytime half-life of afternoon kips. Have spoken to a friend about relaxation techniques etc so am going to give it a go.

Hopefully after a couple of weeks of the odd siesta here and there I will be ready to pull the inevitable all-nighters that H will spring on us, along with G who will probably wake when he hears the screams.

I find it difficult to get to sleep at the best (or most tired!) of times, so may need someone to come round with a big mallet... we'll see what happens...

As it was I was just SO knackered and run down that I put off the rapid return to bed routine... also thinking about it, it makes sense to wait until Steve is back home for good to help me. There is a lot of change coming: Steve finishing work, Christmas, not going to Grandad's house for Christmas for the first time since H was born, relatives coming here...

2nd November 2012
Sleight of hand

And for my next trick...

H loves those yogurt fruit flakes, but often drops one on the floor... or at least he thinks he has.
Cue instructions from Number 2 son: "Mummy get pick up... there..." whilst gesturing at an area of the floor.
Hmm... can't see anything... maybe it's rolled further away...
Suddenly I'm yanked back: "There!!!"
Ok it's right here, somewhere. But actually there isn't anything.
Damn.
I pat the ground with one hand whilst palming a "yogurt fruit sweet" with the other from the table.
Then, with a flourish: "There!"

I'm getting quite good at this sleight of hand thing... now I just need a glamorous assistant...

22nd November 2012
What was the trigger here...?!

Hubby had been away the last couple of weeks doing some training, not coming back at weekends like he usually does. He has now been back a few days during the working week, and he's not usually here on a school night.
I know. I'm afraid I'm going into advanced detective mode with H now to second guess the triggers for his meltdowns.

Well, after dropping the yogurt fruit sweets H got more and more twitchy (behaviourally, not physically) as time went on.
He asked for ridged crisps – I didn't have any, so offered an alternative. Ok. He tried them, but then declined them, offering them back to me saying "Thank you Mummy." These weren't things he hadn't had before by the way.

Anyway, the computer was on, so I offered him one of his favourite bubble pop games. "No, Mummy playing Bubble Witch Saga."
I played the level with him at the table behind me watching. When I lost the game I said it was finished. This is usually acceptable to H, but not this time.
Cue massive meltdown, which to be fair didn't last as long as they have done in the past, but it was quite violent.
Lots of leaping around onto his knees, banging his wrists and head on the floor, pinching Steve's neck, at which point I intervened and pulled him away to try and take him for time out in the other room. Punched me in the face, legs windmilling and madly kicking out. He was really strong, I couldn't control him at all.
After a while he reverted back to Steve to resolve the mood: getting him to do the "rub it better" routine etc, saying "no stop it, yes stop it" as Steve had said this to him earlier when he was hurting himself.
Finally "Daddy lie down with H upstairs." An hour on it's all quiet. I remember that he had a more disturbed night than usual (that's saying something for H as he is up and down like a yo-yo!)
So was this the "dropped" sweet from earlier, not having the ridged crisps, or just being too darn tired and emotional? Or is Daddy home too much?!!
I just don't know.

23rd November 2012
Playing nicely – open wide!

H has spied G chewing on something non-foodie, and is now playing mouth police, trying to get the offending object.
"G get aaahhh...!"
G amazingly complies with a little help from H's prising fingers.
H is contented and wanders off again.
G then starts chasing H, laughing.
The next few minutes are spent with the two running around laughing, stopping for a moment for G to open his mouth in H's face, chasing each other again...

This would have been unimaginable a couple of years ago...

25th November 2012
Broken nose? I hope not!

We are lounging in bed, H has done his usual thing of getting the iPad to play Angry Birds.
"Mummy private!" Oh dear. You're 8, don't start getting an unhealthy obsession...
Me: "What about Mummy's private?!"
H: "Mummy private!" He wants a repeat from me.
Me: "Mummy private? H is funny!"
H, laughing in his cheeky monkey voice: "Private broken!!"
"Private's not broken!"
Touching my face, smiling: "Broken nose... broken mouth... broken eyes..."
Erm... is this his plan for the day?!? Please, no?!
"Kicking private!!" Thankfully not acting this out.
Me in a jokey manner (don't want to set him off!) "H you don't kick Mummy's private!!"

Hmm I wonder if I need to invest in one of those boxes that cricketers wear down their pants... and an American football face shield...

26th November 2012
Playing sensory style

Perhaps this whole "having two kids on the Spectrum" thing could work after all: I mean G actually seems to *like* being repeatedly whacked in the face by a balloon...

And H seems to really like doing it...

27th November 2012
Word play

H's first nocturnal visit was at half 10, an hour and a half since he'd gone to sleep. Two more visits after that, then at 2am he was awake and wanting the ipad.
Not the best night we've ever had! This was the conversation we had at breakfast...

"Mummy pick up the chocolate drink." He is pointing to an empty milkshake bottle on the table next to his hand. It has fallen over.
"Mummy pick up the chocolate drink there."
You know what? After less than 3 hours of broken kip I'm not inclined to argue. I pick up the bottle.
Sue me.

"To-po..."
?? Nope. Don't know where this one has come from.
"To-po!!"
Oh no, we're back on the repeating thing again.
Me: "To-po."
Yeah I know, he's going to be really tired and cranky (a bit like me) so I'm not rocking the boat. "Weh! Meh... meh like a baby!"
Me: "Meh like a baby?!"
"Bear." Ok good rhyming?!
In-between phrases he is flapping his arms up and down, jerking from his wrists as if he's trying to shake his fingers free of something.

H, laughing: "Bear coming to play!!"

28th November 2012
Feeling good

I love singing, and am going through my wardrobe looking for things to wear for a night out with the choir.

"Oh freedom is mine, and I know how I feel...
It's a new dawn, it's a new day, it's a new life... for me...
And I'm feeling goooooooood..."

Yep, the boys are at school, and I'm dancing around the house singing my lungs out. See what 4 hours solid sleep does for a girl!!!

28th November 2012
Helpful H

H seems to be intent on "helping" G to play.
We currently have him wrapping his arms around G's chest from behind and boosting him up, trying to make him "jump."
I suppose that's exercise of a kind for H, and G is still smiling... for now...
Now he is marching G along, ipad in one arm, the other snugged around G's shoulder. Now he's making him clap his hands.
This could go bad quickly, though it's quite nice to see now - will have to watch this one...

Update: the next day I caught H trying to "help" G jump by sticking a half-nelson around his neck and jerking upwards: G had quite a grimace on his face with his eyes screwed shut, but rather alarmingly was quite compliant in this... probably likes being strangled... oh gawd...
I hastily put on my best "jolly" voice saying to H "Not G's neck!"
Didn't really want to precipitate a meltdown while H had the death grip on him. Thankfully he accepted this quite well and went back to gripping G around the chest – phew!

28th November 2012
Strange habits

"Chips and silver spoon."
Too bad we're not having chips. And why would you want to use a spoon??
"Potatoes with silver spoon!"
We're not having potatoes, we're having toast and spicy meat (pepperoni).
"Toast and meat with silver spoon!"

He is now placing squares of toast onto the spoon before eating it.
Oh dear... don't let this be the start of another obsession...

29th November 2012
Balancing act

Really very tired today, but had agreed to meet some other "autism mum" friends.
Am so glad I did, despite this precluding any chance of a catch-up kip.

I am perfecting the balancing act of emotional vs. physical wellbeing.

For now it's ok, though I know the whole lack of sleep thing isn't sustainable in the long term...

Chapter 12

"Well I wish it could be Christmas... every da-a-ay..."

Oh boy. Haven't even got a tree up yet and it's starting...

2nd December 2012 "That most... wonderful time... of the year..."

H has been getting a little more twitchy again lately with the whole repeating sounds thing, wanting me to copy his words exactly. I don't know if it's the whole gearing up to Christmas thing or what. He's also just come back today from a 2 night residential respite break where he was lovely as always. We then went to the playbarn where there was a bunch of particularly boisterous boys whose behaviour he copied; subsequently he upset some little girls, which later caused a mini meltdown from H.

I've been going with the repeating lately to keep things on an even keel, as in other ways he has been so good, playing nicely together with G. It doesn't seem too much to ask to repeat a few things to alleviate his anxiety at this point... though I could change my tune on that one, watch this space!!

Daddy and H have been playing with the train set in the other room. They come into the dining room.

H, a little agitated: "Thomas got hit."

Steve: "Thomas got bumped but it's ok."

No Daddy, wrong answer!!!

"Thomas hurt!!"

Steve: "Thomas isn't hurt!"

No, no, no... still wrong!!

Cue mini meltdown... "Thomas... to-po... oh,oh,oh Thomas, Nik Nak crisps..."

A little later...

"Listen to guitar music."

?!?

Quick, get something up on the internet, a bit of video...

We then had to pause the guitar, play the guitar, pause the guitar...

Next I got some screaming in my face: "Car mud be go..." (or something like that.)

Me, getting a little weary now: "I don't know what you're saying."

"Yes talking!!!"

Me, wearily: "Yes talking."

Whatever.

"Cuddle with Daddy." (Well it did start with Daddy after all.)

Goes and cuddles.

"Daddy lie down with H have happy Christmas music."

Crap. Where's his Christmas CD, haven't seen it for a year. It is only the 2nd of December for crying out loud. Can't find it, manage to find an old freebie carols disk from the newspaper.

I ensconce him in his bed with his ipad and the carols playing. Daddy is then instructed to go upstairs. After a moment Daddy comes down again to find some Nik Nak crisps.

It's all quiet now. Steve is off away again tonight to work for the week so I'm hoping that's the end of it...

4th December 2012 Repeat after me... again...

Things are on the slide a bit... H seems to be making a habit of getting up at 1 or 2am to come into my bed as usual. But instead of going to sleep he's getting the ipad, bringing it back to bed and playing on it until I get up and about after 7am.

He seems to need less and less, but still slept all night as far as I know recently at his residential unit. Today I've been awake since 1.30am listening to my lads chasing, giggling and systematically running down the batteries of 2 iPods and an iPad.

I think I'm the only "low-functioning" one in this household right now... zzz...

Oh God, the trickle of H making me repeat his words and sounds is speeding up lately... I'm hoping it's down to the fact that he was up at 1.30am, only going back to sleep for an hour at school this afternoon. He is increasingly twitchy; again just because he's tired? I can live in hope! He keeps wanting me to repeat nonsense stuff: "Yes talking!!"

Also especially when tired or stressed he starts trying to control me again.

He knocked a packet of crackers off the table when he was flapping about with a toy, but Mummy had to pick it up to forestall full meltdown. After I'd complied and picked up the crackers he contented himself with making me repeat the words "Mummy can pick up the crackers" half a dozen times.

5th December 2012 What's good for one is good for the other... oh wait, it's not...

I've often joked with a friend who also has 2 children on the spectrum about the possibility of forgetting which strategy you're using for which child. I did something similar here: reading the same non-verbal cues from H that I get from G about having a new nappy, when that wasn't what H wanted at all!

So this morning G has laid down in the usual place for me to do his nappy and change him for school. H then comes along and lies down too. Oh ok, it's earlier than usual but I'll sort you out too. Well that's fine, he goes back to the table (iPad in hand, naturally) and munches on his cereal bar and fruit.

Right, fast forward. G has gone off to school on the bus and H and I are ready to go, just need to put his socks and shoes on last thing.

H lies down again: "Trousers off again, nappy off again."

Oh crap. I did it in the wrong order didn't I! He usually eats first then we get changed. I can't be doing with the paddy that will emerge so after a bit of a grumble I do it.

"Pyjamas off again." (He means his shirt and jumper.)

Oh for goodness sake, right, ok, ok...

We're sorted. I leave a message with the school to say we're going to be late.

Again.

Me: "H sit on the big chair put socks on."

He complies, then says "socks off again!" straight away.

Nope, I've had enough. There should be no re-set required for the socks, we've only just put them on!

Cue screaming session. I walk away into the next room. I can hear all the banging.

Me: "Whatever H!" Not really helpful I know but I'm quite stressed too ok?!

He then comes in asking for cuddles, saying "Bang your head" asking me to rub it better etc. I manage to calm him down slightly before he asks me to turn the ipad off: "Mummy can get ipad turn it off!"

All right.

"Mummy can get ipad turn it on!!"

Oh here we go again! Nope. Not starting all that again either, where I might as well say "Yes sir, no sir, 3 bags full sir!"

More screaming, more cuddling.

On the way to school I'm sure he's remembering another meltdown from before.

"Disk at old home." He means the DVD player at our old house.

Me: "Old home finished."

H: "Disk broken at old home."

Me: "Yes, the disk was broken at old home."

This seems to be the end of it, let's hope he's not all anxious when he comes home.

It could have been much, much worse, but it's stressful enough; and I really feel like we're regressing here, back into the ritualistic behaviours.

8th December 2012
Different approaches

All four of us are at the supermarket. (I know, I can practically hear the squeals of protest from my purse...) Steve lets G out of the car then proceeds to root around in the car for something. I'm with G, it's ok... oh now Steve has already let H out... but he's still faffing...
Right H has dodged by me and is running off towards the shop entrance, ipad tucked into his arm.
I yell at Steve to keep an eye on G, he says yes that's fine but strangely doesn't come to me to put a hand on G. This is the one that usually does runners remember?!
H despite my yelling is not slowing down in his bid for escape... I'm stood with an arm on G, unwilling to let him have the freedom of the car park, and yell at hubby again: "Have you got G?!" I get rather a grumpy reply to the affirmative but a tortoise would be moving quicker to get to G! I find it hard to cut the invisible thread linking me to G but hubby doesn't seem to have the same sense of urgency...

Finally I'm free to sprint after a gleeful H, catching him up at the entrance where he plonks himself in a trolley.
He then proceeds to whine, prompting me to say "it's all right H" a few times. This is in response to my obvious agitation and statements that he mustn't run away from Mummy.
The next few minutes I spend pushing the trolley round doubled over H, while his arms are gripped around my neck. His latest thing is to take a leaf out of G's book, but amend it slightly. G's speciality is the hand gouge: targeting the tendons on the back of your hand. H has perfected the head grind: squeezing you ultra tight whilst forcing our skulls together. It's uncomfortable, but not as painful as the hand gouge so I'm thankful for small mercies.

9th December 2012
Advent calendar

So hubby has bought a lovely wooden advent calendar with a nativity scene on top. Each day you pull open a little door to take out the next character. Steve has been a little confused by what H thought was in the drawer.

Number 7 is a shepherd.
H: "Woodcutter!"
??
Number 8 H finds a sheep: "Sheep!" Yes. Well done!
Number 9 H finds a...
"Cinderella!"
No...
"Woodcutter!"
No... it's another shepherd...

We've been doing fairy tales at school then...

9th December 2012
Hanging up clothes

"H hanger!!"
He comes in with a clothes hanger shoved down the back of his jumper.
Right concept.
Wrong application.

10th December 2012
"Here comes Santa Claus, here comes Santa Claus..."

Hubby has got a bit carried away with the whole "Christmas in our own house" thing. Well, only a little. There are just a couple of little colourful signs saying "Noel" and "Joy." Never mind that the lights criss-crossing the ceiling in the hallway look like Santa's grotto.

H: "Father Christmas Joy."
Me: "Father Christmas Joy? The sign says Joy."
H: "Father Christmas tomorrow!"
Me: "That's not right!!"
H: "Father Christmas home tomorrow!!"

Oh boy. No, no..!

10th December 2012
A balanced diet

Three or four years ago G's diet comprised of 5 set foods, all of which were dry, crunchy and salty. He would periodically drop one or two of these foods; I would then desperately trawl the cracker and crisp aisles in the supermarkets hunting for a replacement, which we might stumble on a week later. I remember when he stopped eating BBQ flavour Pringles, which had been a favourite food I could rely on. He had already dropped breadsticks (another one of his staple foods) so I was quite stressed already.

At this time he had the additional diagnosis of "failure to thrive" – not a very nice thing to read about your child. The professionals involved said we had a couple of options: one was to medicate him with Respiridone. This was an anti-psychotic drug usually given to people with schizophrenia. It also had the side effect of increased weight gain, which is why they wanted G to go on it. The other option was to put a gastro tube into his stomach. I really didn't want to go down that route.

I guess I didn't realise just quite how stressed I was until I lost the plot and had yet another proud Mummy moment… yes, that was sarcasm. G had stopped eating the Pringles in preference to just licking the salt off, one by one. I suddenly found myself in tears trying to force the crisps into his mouth. All I could think about was the tube they were talking about putting in his stomach.

His weight is still closely monitored, and his diet is still really limited, but some of the things he eats now we couldn't have thought about a few years ago.

G always surprises me when he finds a new food. He invariably discovers these things in the burnt on deposits of festering unwashed oven trays, or in this case the dish of peelings waiting to go to the compost bin. Now, after I found him gnawing on a piece of rind we have melon to add to his menu.

See, I knew there was an upside to being such a crap housewife!

No wonder he has a strong constitution for one so under-nourished.

13th December 2012
Normal kind of conversation

Communicating with the young one:
"Mummy faces up. H faces up.
Up on the ceiling. H climbing ceiling.
Don't climb on ceiling it would break it!!"

The usual requests are fairly brusque and to the point: "Mummy get drink."
Me: "What do you say?"
H: "Drink please!"
Today: "Mum please I get you drink in table H?"
Trying to do a whole sentence out of the blue - bless!

"Where's he gone? Soup? H eat mangos... Monkey eat mangos... H eat mandarin!"
I... nope. I don't know what that was!

14th December 2012
"Santa Claus is coming to town..." again...

H: "Father Christmas another time, Father Christmas coming to play!"
Me: "Father Christmas isn't coming to play, that's funny!"
"H laughing ho ho ho! Father Christmas coming soon..."
Oh dear...
Me: "Father Christmas coming wait and see." Arrgh...
H: "Wait and see Father Christmas..." phew... ok...
Then: "Father Christmas coming tomorrow...!"
Help!!!

14th December 2012 "I'll be home for Christmas..." (Sorry, getting carried away with the Christmas songs!)

Well that's it. After over 2 and a half years of being a weekend hubby and Dad preceded by 4 months serving overseas, Steve is out of the RAF and home for good. (We hope!) We'll see if things get easier or harder! Hopefully the former... it'll certainly be nice to escape more to a quiet mattress somewhere away from H's nocturnal visits!

Annie and I have got into quite a routine during the week, but hopefully hubby and I will settle back into being together full time.

Let's see how long the honeymoon period lasts!

15th December 2012
A trip to town... calmer times

The scale on the stress monitor for going around town seems to be easing ... (quick, touch wood!!) or maybe I'm just getting better at managing it all...

Generally these days we have to obey the shop signs. For instance when in the "WHSmith shop" we have to go straight away to find something with WHSmith on. Then we're ok. Followed hubby into somewhere called "The Tool Shop" without realising the name. H however kept telling me to "pick up the two..." pointing at some reels of tape on the shelf.

Me: "It's tape, Mummy pick up the tape." I suddenly realised he was referring to "The Tool Shop" name printed on the price tags.

Oh...

Later, a police car goes by, siren wailing.

"H didn't play in the fire!!"

It's ok lad, I know you didn't do anything wrong!

15th December 2012
H's jokes

H asks for an ice cream, I tell him he's already had an ice cream, and that too much ice cream makes you sick.

H: "Hiccup sick!" He does a hiccup.

Me: "No sick, just hiccups."

H: "Spit poo!!"

Me, laughing: "Poo is poo, spit is spit!"

H: "Spitty spit poo!!"

16th December 2012
Party!!

Well we took the boys to their first mainstream kids party in... well in about 9 years!
Apart from G prising a sweet from a little girls fingers it all went lovely. Of course it helps if said party is arranged by some mates of yours who are willing to spin, dance, chase and generally round up your kids!

17th December 2012
Identifying sounds...

Going to school this morning they had a guy on the radio who was a champion whistler or something. Before whistling a Christmas song you could hear him preparing... frankly it sounded like he was eating with his mouth open...
H: "Cat licking!!"

17th December 2012
Changes?

So I was talking with hubby today after dropping H off at school. I know, it's a novelty he's actually here having breakfast with me! We were suddenly thinking about how H doesn't throw things any more. Correction. Hasn't thrown things for a while!
Generally, things are getting slowly more manageable again. It can't be Steve being home cos he's only just finished work. A slight shift in behaviour has snuck by me un-noticed, it's kind of been a slow drip-feed.

A few things:
When dragging G around by the neck, H is now more able to release him without meltdown when I say "Not G's neck!" It's a good thing

G has been patient enough to put up with this rough-housing as it's given H the time to slowly adjust to the way he should be handling him. He still needs the prompt from me, but, you know; baby steps.

The playbarn: months of going in saying "Play nicely in the playbarn!" seems to have helped a little; H's response is always "Don't want to touch the children on the big slide!!"

Swishing water in the bath: H likes to whoosh his bum up and down the bath creating a tidal wave that slops over onto the carpet. (I know, carpet in the bathroom, I blame the previous owners.) Hubby said to him: "H don't do that, that's naughty." (Gasp, I know, the N word!!) H thought about it for a bit then said "Don't want the water to fall!"

But this was what really woke me up to it... lo and behold, this morning Steve changed H's nappy and clothes before sitting him at the table to eat. The dreaded words came: "H need new nappy!" As before I told him that he'd already had a new nappy, and guess what? No meltdown!!!

18th December 2012
Boundaries!

Well, so after hubby has been working away from home for a while, he is back for good. Straightaway the boys go and pull an all-nighter!
Welcome home!!
(Sorry, did that sound a little bit smug?!)

After this disturbed night I'm kipping on a mattress on the floor to escape the H syndrome. I'm in a dressing room area off the side of the bedroom so have still been a little disturbed by the nocturnal activities – nothing like Steve has though!
I'm half asleep when I slowly become aware of somebody gently stroking each side of my body from my top down to my legs and back.
Oh husband, for God's sake, aren't you tired...? And G is down by my feet...

Shit!! G is down by my feet, eww, arrgh, it's G, get off - not appropriate!!

It's at times like this you're glad you sleep on your front.
Note to self, if I'm somewhere accessible to the kids, wear pj's.

19th December 2012
"Bear!"

H has been strangely attached to a toy bear since being so tired yesterday morning. It even had to go to school to say hello to his TA before going back to the car with me when I left him. This was the concession I made to him after he requested "bear at school!"
The bear almost (gasp) superseded the ipad this morning!!

Oh, he also wore a Santa hat all night.

19th December 2012
Emotional times

Hubby has gone back to his old work for a couple of days for a Christmas do.

H is trying to force-feed G the crisps that G requested then discarded. I look at G and say "it's all right G" as he extricates himself from H's clutches.
H: "G doesn't eat star crisps." (They are star shaped ok?!)
No, G doesn't eat star crisps.
"G doesn't eat star crisps!" Kind of stressy now.
I have to repeat this a couple more times. Then H puts his arms around my neck and starts crying.
H: "H don't be crying!"
Me: "Is H sad?"
H: "H don't be sad."

20ᵗʰ December 2012
Talking to Mummy

H: "Hear the Christmas lights outside."
Hmm is this mis-communication? Or evidence of a superpower that I don't possess?!

Meanwhile the speechless one is with me, vocalising: "Did-dee-ahh... did-dee-ahh..."
G is smiling at me letting me hold his hand. I stroke his face. He's still got the softest cheeks in the world, even from when he was a baby...

20ᵗʰ December 2012
Normal stuff...

So I volunteer to make some mince pies for a community thing at the Thrift shop. That's fine, all is going well. I have to wait in for some furniture to arrive anyway; they'll send a text message an hour before it comes so no need to worry about the school run. Mince pies are done, cooling on the oven.
Am just going to get H from school when you guessed it: ding dong!
I'm supposed to be picking H up at 3. By the time they finish assembling the sofas it's 5 past. It would be fine if I didn't have to be back home in 25 minutes, but now I can't get H. Have been making frantic phone calls to friends to get G, but no-one's free. Finally get through to H's after school club and book him in until 5pm. Phew. Somebody just tell his TA who's already waiting for me please?! I was supposed to be at the Thrift with the mince pies at 5pm but never mind will have to be late.
Hm, right, must do something with the mince pies before G gets back.

Ding dong!
Oh, now it's the firewood delivery 45 minutes early. Ok.
So I'm busy trying to stack wood in the rain as quickly as possible when G gets back. It's so cold and wet I can't feel my fingers.

Arrgh, quick! I just manage to claw the tray of mince pies from G's grasp before he does any damage. He's happy with the burnt on dribbled out bits of mincemeat though. Mm...tasty!

Right, lock them away. Back to the wood, I haven't finished stacking it yet. A cubic metre is a surprisingly large amount, getting slightly knackered. My fingers actually hurt now... sod it. The rest will just have to get wet.

Damn, so busy stacking wood it's only 20 minutes until I have to leave to get H. Bollocks, will have to get KFC drive through later.

I've still got another set of mince pies to do. Hmm... might go to Tesco instead...

Right, sort a snack for G in the meantime and get a bag ready for when we're at the Thrift.
Oh lord, I forgot about the icing sugar that was left out...!

At least I don't have to think too hard whether G's uniform will last until tomorrow... he looks like he's been let loose in a flour mill.
Why do I do these things on a day when Annie can't help and Steve isn't here?!

3 hours later...

Well I guess it was all a little too much.
H's day today consisted of:
School, Christmas dinner, party, after school club, Thrift shop, library, KFC drive through, home.

All fine until the boys were sitting having their dinner and H upped and whacked G across the face. This happened so fast I'm not sure what prompted it, but after some detective work I think I have it. H often takes exception to G twiddling with stuff, I thought at first this was it.
It appears now though that it was a brown sauce issue. I had given H one of the sachets from the shop, but when he asked for more Steve gave him sauce from a bottle we had. (He was home by the evening, as you can see.)

We have now had to clean off the old brown sauce, add more on, put it all on a different plate etc.

So this is how it went:

H has a sachet of brown sauce, asks for more. Daddy gets bottled sauce instead. H then asked for red sauce, Steve went to try and find it, couldn't, asked me.

I found a sachet of red sauce put it on the second plate that hubby had supplied.

G twiddled some lettuce.

H whacked G in the face.

Steve yelled at H.

H screamed and started bashing himself and us.

G cried.

I took H upstairs where he threw stuff around, hit himself and me.

I told him to calm down, got hit some more.

I laid crossways across his body and arms so he couldn't hit us any more. (No, I didn't squash him.)

H: "Off, ow, ow!!!" (I wasn't crushing him ok?!)

I left him in the room. He ran out: "H downstairs with Mummy!!"

Proceeded to try and kick me down the stairs.

More leaping around onto his knee caps etc.

2 hours later we had finished calming down though we were still on high alert status, and he went to bed.

So it could have been a lot worse!

I know, I know, there was WAY too much going on that day!

21st December 2012
Fun and games

H: "Ceiling clouds... ceiling outside!"

Me: "That's not right, ceiling's are in houses!"

H: "That's not right, that's not the words!"

23rd December 2012
Something is going on...

Last year, in the world according to H, a house with loads of lights on was "Christmas Day." I'm really hoping nobody mentions it this year as that place is in a different county! We'll just stick to "December 25" in our house.

Last year H couldn't grasp the concept of "Christmas Day." Today he has obviously heard "Christmas Eve" mentioned.
Ok, here goes.
Me: "December 24 is called Christmas Eve."

I think we might be ok...?

24th December 2012
"Twas the night before Christmas..."

Granddad, Aunty and Uncle have "come to play" for several days over Christmas.
G was at the carer's when they arrived – you should've seen the big smile on his face when he saw them. Almost like it was Christmas!! We only see them intermittently in the school holidays so it's a real treat for us and the boys.

We have all gone on the ferry to town. We only took one buggy so the boys are taking it in turns to walk. G is starting to refuse to walk so it's his turn in the buggy. We decide to go in some shops to look for pyjamas for them.
In one place there isn't much so we come out, when I hear the dreaded words: "Mummy   get   pay   the   lady!"
Me: "We didn't buy anything, no paying the lady today."
H: "Pay the lady closed!"

And guess what? That was it - no meltdown!! Happy Christmas!

25th December 2012
Christmas Day

8am

I don't have the whole worry about Santa and presents. H comes down to the lounge where I'm sleeping on the floor, there's a load of presents under the tree.

Who cares about them – there's a chocolate selection box with the words helpfully printed on to tell us what's inside!!

"Open chocolate selection box please!"

9.30am

"Peach on face."

Peach on face??

"H is a fruit!!"

Me: "H is a fruit?! You're funny!!"

Honey we're all fruitcakes in this house...

"Toilet tomorrow at playbarn!"

Oh dear, wait and see! (We are *not* going to the playbarn!!)

H: "26 is called Christmas Eve."

Me: "December 24 is called Christmas Eve."

"26 is called bee dee dee dee deee!"

What?!?

"26 tomorrow."

No, I'm not even going there on the whole Boxing Day thing.

H: "Car tomorrow. Shop tomorrow. Seaside tomorrow..."

10am

This is the first Christmas that we haven't spent at Grandad's house. H has been asking me about going there for a few months now, as we didn't go at half term either...

H: "Grandad's house is closed, Grandad's house is a long way away, Granddad's house another time... too busy for Granddad's house..."

Bless him.

1 pm
Daddy, Grandad and Uncle have taken G out in the car, in a desperate bid to find medicine for Steve's cold. When they get back G hunkers down on the kitchen floor next to my feet. How lovely to be able to command some of those extra pairs of hands to entertain him while my sister-in-law and I carry on cooking.

2pm
Lunch: G is actually sitting at the table. My sister-in-law has been overly optimistic and put roast potato, sweet potato and carrot on his plate along with some green beans, sweetcorn and stuffing. He's ignoring it of course, though on the plus side he's snaffling cranberry and apple chipolatas from the serving dish on the table. And no, despite them disappearing from his plate there are no offending half chewed bits on the floor under his chair: amazing!

3pm
Hubby has taken the boys out for a walk, so it's quite peaceful here. How different it is to a normal day when you haven't usually got other people here too.

4pm
I'm feeling festive now, have just got a fire going in the woodburner, and G is rubbing my bare feet over his face.
It's quite soothing actually.

5.30pm
Right, H has got the whole thing where a certain date is called something: "December 24 is called Christmas Eve."
He also seems to think December 25 is called Christmas Eve, and December 26 is called "Christmas Dee dee dee dee dee!!!"

So now I've corrected him as well as I can and hallelujah I think we've got it: December 24 = Christmas Eve, December 25 = Christmas Day, December 26 = Christmas Boxing Day.
Well yes I know it's just Boxing Day, but no matter how I put it he wouldn't accept that Boxing Day didn't have the same prefix as the others.
That's ok though, I like it, sounds more festive anyway!

6.30pm

A lovely and rare sight: G and H sitting side by side on the armchair behind Grandad laughing and giggling together. I grab the camera. When I'm looking at the photo evidence later I'm struck by how far our lads have come. All those repetitions of "Gentle to G" must have paid off a little after all!

8pm

Well I think I might be my Mother's daughter after all... hubby is out driving the boys around, my visitors are watching telly in the lounge, and I am sitting here roasting in front of the fire feeding the flames: firebug!!

26th December 2012
Christmas Boxing Day

I was kipping downstairs on the floor until I heard our little resident furry friend scratching around the room – I really must put those mouse traps down. Anyway I heard H do his visit to our bed so I nipped upstairs into his. Later on again this morning I did a bit more bed hopping to end up in my own lovely, comfy, memory foam bed... aaaah...

H has come to wake me up...

"Number 26 is called...?"
Me: "Number 26 is called Boxing Day."
H: "Christmas Boxing Day."
Yes that's right.
H: "Number 27 is called...?"
Me: "Number 27 is called number 27."
H: "Number 28 is called...?"
Me: "Number 28 is called number 28." Ok stop now.
H: "Number 29 is called...?"
Me: "Number 29 is called number 29!" Sigh.
H: "Number 30 is called...?" Oh boy. You get the picture.
H: "Number 31 is called...?" Hmm... do I, don't I? Ok I'm going for it...
Me: "December 31 is called New Year's Eve." Done it now.

Pause.
H chuckling: "Number 27 is called Christmas Boxing Day!!!"

Can we go back to just having the dates please?!

Steve is doing some work in the garden, G joins him.
It's a lovely sunny day as G walks up and down the length of the car running his tongue along the bodywork...

2pm

I'm more exhausted than I have a right to be really. I mean we do have visitors here at the moment, helping with the day to day running of the boys' lives. Nappies, meals, walks etc. But that's probably the reason why, isn't it. I mean your mind's now telling your body: "It's ok, relax. Help is here!" There's less to stress about so I'm in catch up mode again.
We're in the car now, driving off to buy some curtains for the poor bare dining room window. But that's ok, cos there's 3 more adults on hand to push buggies and run interference with the boys. Hmm, feeling sleepy... the car is very warm... what soothing music...

27th December 2012
Meltdown with Daddy

I've decided to start off in our bed with hubby and just sneak out when H comes in and nip into his. Not keen on kipping on the floor downstairs with the mouse running loose...

12.30am

Took a sleeping tablet half an hour ago. I'm just about to turn out the light when H comes in and flomps down on top of the duvet. He's sparked out. A bit of man-handling, we get him under the duvet and I drag off to H's bed with my hot water bottle.

?am

Screaming, banging, screaming, what's going on? Ugh, shouldn't have had that sleeping pill. Ok now Steve's cursing at H. Oh dear.
"Daddy get downstairs with H!!!"

Hmm... I think they've gone... must close my eyes...

Apparently H was asking for "pamper-tor" which totally flummoxed Steve. He eventually took a guess and took his temperature with the digital thermometer – much to H's bemusement.

28th December 2012
Bear: the new twin

H is getting a little obsessed with "Bear."
So I was putting H to bed, we were mid-Gruffalo story when: "Bear!"
Right. Got Bear and put him in bed next to H. Started reading again.
"Santa hat Mummy and Daddy's room!"
Ok. I try to take H's Santa hat off. Yes he was wearing it to bed again. I'm meeting some resistance.
"Santa hat Mummy and Daddy's room!!"
Oh, right, I get ya.
I go to our room and find the other Santa hat which we then have to put on Bear. H then proceeds to faff with the duvet, trying to tuck it equally under Bear's and his own chin correctly.

Roll on Christmas and any related paraphernalia finishing in January.

29th December 2012
Missing you already...

After staying nearly a week, Grandad, Auntie and Uncle have gone home.

"See Grandad, Auntie and Uncle on December 30."
Me: "See Grandad in April."
"See Grandad at Grandad's house on April."

Father / son bonding

Steve is tickling G's neck, making silly "tickling" noises: "dee dee dee dee...!"

G immediately mimics the sound, his face coming alight with a huge smile. Then a second time: the grin becoming a tight concentrated grimace, his fingers flicking furiously in front of his eyes...
Happy moments of Father / son bonding.

Map man

We have been for a cup of tea at the café near the woods. It's too wet and muddy for a walk so we decide on a little drive instead, listening to the radio.
We turn left out of the car park instead of right.
Immediately: "We're going to old home!"
No!
He's looking at the routes in his mind again... I wonder if he's got something like the London Underground Tube map in his head...?

30th December 2012
Lazy Sunday

4pm
This... is just unheard of...! Just the 4 of us here, hubby doing jobs, lads on and off of trampoline and cuddling on the sofa with me - separately naturally - we have spent the WHOLE day at home so far with no meltdowns!
Am about to go out now for the drive I promised H.
The question is, do I change out of my pyjamas!?

Ok, I actually took the other option: hubby has taken them out and I'm catching up on Downton Abbey on telly. I'm going to hell!!

31st December 2012
"Christmas New Year's Eve" – Happy New Year!

10.30am
Well it's New Year's Eve and all that. Each day is a new one though. So far this morning I have chilled with G stroking my feet, and given H a squeezy hug prior to him running up and down the room squealing with excitement.

Happy Monday everyone!!

11.30am
H: "Hello."
Me: "Hello!"
H, with a big smile and a hug: "Oh I love you... SO much!!"

How lucky am I!

H is now singing Auld Lang Syne. It goes a bit like this:
"Should bold... da bee doo beee... ba doo..."

12 noon
Steve has been out with the boys in the car and they've just come back. He comes in the back door with H, but H is getting quite agitated.
"Daddy can shut the door... another hand!!"
I tell Steve to just repeat what H says as he is now really fretting. He has shoved Steve outside and wants him to stay out while shutting the door. But H wants him to use his left hand, not his right.
Hubby is trying to do this, and is repeating what H says, but obviously he's not doing stuff correctly.
H goes into the dining room and throws the ipod he's holding a couple of times. Steve tries to calm him but is shoved back to the kitchen, back to the back door: "Daddy get back!"
Oops

Finally Steve does everything right, closes the door correctly, and gives me an enquiring look from outside. I give a little shrug in return. It's too late though, H can't cope any more. Hopefully we can start to "re-set" though.
After a couple of seconds H starts punching himself in the head, Hubby comes in again. I can only watch. Whatever upset him, it was started by Steve and therefore must be sorted out by Steve.
H is asking for cuddles from Daddy, who is responding, whilst half his attention is on pottering and putting bits away. Arrgh! Not helping! I tell him that H needs his full attention during this calming down phase, or his behaviour will escalate again.

Half an hour later H is cuddling with me on my bed. He's still a little fragile I can tell. Here's the conversation we had...

"Dee dee dee dee..."

?? I repeat everything he says – naturally!

"Making that words, dee dee dee dee!"

Oh right!

The same format is followed for his other words...

"Set toe! Making that words, set toe!"

"What's at hop! Making that words, what's at hop!"

Me: "I like cuddling with you!"

H: "A light light..."

He's now trying to mimic me, but has misheard / misunderstood me again!

"Don't be scared, don't be scared... making a sentence... doggy..."

"Spider and dog and cat and bird and horse..."

"H magnert...?"

Me: "Do you mean magnet??"

"Magnet!"

Me: "I see..."

"I see with magnet!!"

He's snuggled into my body, playing with the ipod. I get cuddles from H but not for such long periods. These are my "stealth cuddles" from the young one. I can stick my arm around him and endlessly squeeze... I don't want to move...

"Dobbling H."

?? Really, I wish I knew what was going on in his head!

"I think so dobbling H... dobbling pop... dobbling pop H..."

"H walk on ceiling, possible ceiling, possible sky..." (He means *im*possible to walk on sky. At least I think so...)

"Tone boast at new home. Flash like a dog." (Splash like a dog?? I'm lost!!)

He's now fiddling with my toes.

"Toes toes toes toes toes!! Too's!! Jungle jungle jungle... there's no such thing says H... there's no such thing says Mummy!"

Ok not so much a conversation as H just bamboozling me with the contents of his head!!

1.30pm

Everything's nice and calm now. I've promised H he can play a game on the computer before we go out. I'm just settling him down at the desk in the dining room while Steve is clattering around in the kitchen cupboards.

I hear a faint hiss under Steve's breath: "Fu.... sss...."

H immediately pipes up: "Fucks sake with Mummy?"

Ahem.

Moving on.

1.40pm

I'm upstairs looking out clothes from the drawers. G has grabbed my foot and is gleefully rubbing his chin over my heel.

I think he must have been a cat in a former life...

9pm

I've done a few New Year's Eve shindigs in my time, drinking copious amounts of booze.

Now though, it's more about reclining back on the sofa with hubby, watching telly and having a last-ditch attempt to fill out my fat pants by eating my own weight in lard!

Because after all, any night can be "party night" here with the boys: you have to preserve energy while you can!

5th January 2013
"Christmas finished!"

Well I did worry about when to stop the whole Christmas thing. Was going to take the decorations down on 1st January, but as it was still a holiday according to H, New Year's Day was "Christmas New Year's Day!!" He was also going on about January 2 being Xmas New Year's Boxing Day - arrgh!!

Finally settled on doing the 12 days of Christmas. Now January 5 equals "Christmas finished."

That was all fine, we put everything away in the boxes. A couple of days later Sgt H from the Christmas police did find a couple of homemade star pictures from school: "Christmas finished!!" Apart from that everything went smoothly – hurray!

6th January 2013
Together again

I think it's finally sinking in, the hubby being back for good. Sunday evening and my 3 fellas have gone out for a drive, while I've actually stayed home and am cooking a proper dinner! No fried chicken from the drive through while hubby packs up his gear ready for his 3 hour drive... that's all done with. Trouble is, when it's not just you at night, you feel able to have a cheeky glass or two... and I have still got that bottle of port, hmm... and the ginger wine...

Decisions, decisions...

Chapter 13

The world didn't end – we're still here!!

21ˢᵗ December 2012 was supposed to be the end of the world according to Nostradamus. Our first real Christmas in our own home with a "Christmas aware" H was ok too. There was the odd stressful moment it's true, but it was actually very nice!

7th January 2013
Morning chat

I'm lying in bed with the young one.
"Foot broken Mummy... foot broken would get hurt... got my toes!!"
Yes you have, my love. Please don't snap anything!!

Love
"Mwa...   mwa...   blowing   me   kisses!!"
Next thing you know he's planting a big smacker on my lips:
"Mmmmmmmwaaaah!!!"

And he has learned this from the game I play with our non-verbal one.
Autistic? Not affectionate? Pah!

Playing so nicely

Have made the leap of faith; we now have both boys in the back of the car together. We've had them separated due to H attacking G when he did something "wrong" – one in the back, one in the front. Things have been a little better on the H attacking G front though so thought we'd be brave.
And to be honest I'm fed up of being stuck in the back!!

There is lots of giggling going on in the back of the car: "Roast beef... tick, tick, tick!!!"
G is repeatedly putting his hand out, H playing "This little piggy" with his fingers; running his own spidery fingers over G's knees, arms and head.
Then we hear from H: "Doy-ee-ooh, doy-ee-ooh!!"
This is part of G's vocabulary that he is mimicking; it's so lovely to hear them laughing and "talking" together, really enjoying playing together.

9th January 2013
Learning to talk (ish)

"Eat Mummy!"
Me: "You can't eat Mummy!"
"Mummy is not a food... eating Mummy it would might hurt..."
Too right it would!
I'm not sure if he's fantasising about biting me, but I'm thankful that he seems to know it wouldn't be a good thing!

10th January 2013
The issue of getting H to stay in bed all night: cue hysterical laughter!

I have talked myself in and out of doing this in so many different ways, so many times. I've discussed it with the OT (hence the social story), friends who also have autistic children, friends with neurotypical children, Annie, who after me probably knows how to deal with H's problem behaviour better than anyone...

What do I do? H's language vs understanding is still out of kilter with ours… and he only needs something to happen one time to make a ritual out of it…

Do I:

1. Use the social story that copies his current bedtime folder (under the duvet, disk on, close your eyes etc), with the added bit that Mummy and Daddy will be happy if H stays in his own room.
2. Same as number 1, but also saying that if he gets up in the night no-one will talk to him, so as not to give him any feedback, you understand – not because we are actually nasty people or anything.
3. Tell him he doesn't come out until the "bell" (alarm clock goes off) at 7am for example. But then I can foresee H saying "Mummy get bell…" (he's not daft you know) also *having* to have the same time every day, isn't that making things even more rigid…?

   I feel like I'm on a precipice not knowing which way to jump, because frankly, once you commit to something, and it's not right, it'll take ages to rectify… arrgh… what to do… what to do…??

4. Sod it. No prep. Cold turkey. Just do it.

11th January 2013
Operation Bedtime: D Day

Well this doesn't bode well.

Despite apparently sleeping well H really did not want to get up this morning. Lots of requests for sleep, and "Mummy, Daddy and H sleep in Mummy and Daddy's bed." Hmm… do you think he knows what's coming? He got a glimpse of the social story yesterday that says about everybody sleeping in their own beds.

I'm thinking: can we get through this without descending into meltdown, just keep it on a sort of even keel? Or just refuse now and suffer the consequences?

Maybe it was foolish but I decided on the former, trying to divert away from the edge of impending meltdown.

Next: loads of controlling OCD-like behaviour. "No trousers on, Daddy get trousers there... no, there!!" (he means put them 6 inches to the right.) Screaming, punching himself in the head, wanting Daddy to repeat every word he says, wanting temperature taken, new nappy again, Angry Birds trousers on. (Eh? We don't have any?!?)

After 40 minutes of being puppeteered by the young one, getting us to lie down in bed, get his breakfast in bed, (I know, but trust me resistance was futile on this!!) H demanding "sleep" at every opportunity, I lost my rag.

Yes it's been a while I know, but we were in a crazy cycle of acceding to H's obsessions, getting nowhere fast.

I yanked him out of bed, saying "Downstairs... school!"

Lots more screaming while I carefully negotiated those narrow stairs sat down on my bum, trying to coax him after me.

Told you a bungalow would've been a good idea...

A few moments of him sat intensely hammering his heels on the stairs with a combo of flailing arms followed. He was half dressed at this point. I was getting him out of the door to go to the car when he decided he needed his school trousers on.

Eventually we get him in the car fully dressed 10 minutes after he should've been at school. Normally it's a 20 minute drive, I'm hoping the screaming and thrashing will stop soon as hubby isn't used to driving with this going on. It can sap your powers of concentration quite badly; really hope he gets there safely.

10am

Well of course once they were in the car driving to school, H calmed down as usual.

Steve said to the teaching assistant if he kicks off call us and we'll pick him up. Will we?!! Why, why! Seriously, H likes school and the routine and I really don't want to start a precedent where he kicks off and magically gets to go home...

In the meantime I have called the learning disability support team and am waiting for them to get back to me with some top tips for tonight's operation bedtime. After this morning I guess I want some reassurance from the 2 psychologists there that my approach to this problem is going to be the correct one...

Honestly I don't know my arse from my elbow anymore!!

3.30pm

The young one is chatting away again on the way home from school:

"H is a friend, H has friends at school... Marianne is a friend at school..."

Me: "Marianne isn't a friend at school, Marianne is a friend... (erm...) at home!"

H: "Marianne is a friend at Marianne's house!!"

Takes a breath:

"Ceiling clouds, ceiling outside."

Me: "That's not right, ceilings are in houses!"

H: "That's not right, that's not the word..."

Repeat, repeat... my brain hurts!

6pm

Well the psychologist called me back. She was really good I guess at giving me the validation to go ahead and try the bedtime thing if I'm ready, but not to stress about it. Tis true, he's been doing this for years now, a couple more weeks making sure it's really right won't make much difference.

I've made up my mind though, we've got a week to try it, and then a weekend to recover when H goes to respite. And if it doesn't work, it doesn't work. There's no point getting even more stressed about it all. After all, as she pointed out, saying something in clinic is very different to implementing it in the home.

Possible lightbulb moment!

I also know what's going on here a bit I think.

H: "Mummy sleep in Mummy and Daddy's bedroom."

I've been sleeping downstairs to get a break from H's night time visits, he saw me come out of the room again this morning, then started saying about "H sleep with Mummy and Daddy in Mummy and Daddy's bedroom."

Is this starting to upset him?

Well it's been a few weeks that Daddy has been back for good and I've been permanently downstairs, I guess it's possible that unsettled him. After all, the norm for the last 2 or 3 years is me in the bedroom during the week on my own, Daddy in the bedroom at the weekend on his own!

11th January 2013
A direct answer... no, really!

If you only knew how unusual this was...!

"Playbarn on Sunday."
Erm... not sure...
"Playbarn on Sunday wait and see. Playbarn on Sunday! Playbarn on Sunday wait and see! *Playbarn on Sunday!!!*"
Oh dear...
"Does H want to go to the playbarn on Sunday?"

Pause.
"Yes."

Ahhh... bless!!!

12th January 2013
Operation Bedtime: Night 1

So here we are. I've started "Operation Bedtime" - constantly returning H back to his own bed, the idea being that eventually he will give up highjacking the marital bed and my hubby and I can actually sleep together again. Well, we can hope.
The door exit sensors are primed, the bleeper handset by my pillow, notebook by the bed to document times and talking. (If any!)
Let battle commence!

2.20am
Bzzz bzzz... beep-eep-eep beeeep beeeep beep-eep-eep!!!
Off goes the alarm... game on...

Well so much for me not speaking: H really wanted me to parrot after him: "Under the duvet!" I just went with it I'm afraid.
Then just: "Mummy can shut the door, night Mummy."
Ok.

3.43 am

Bzzz...
H came in, I got out of bed and met him.
"Hello! H must sleep in H's bedroom!"
That was him talking, not me!

5 ish (couldn't even be bothered to look at the clock this time!)

Bzzz...
Oh all right... press H's room on the bleeper again to cancel the noise... accept... yes...

I wake later to find a lump under the duvet. Sometime in the last hour G has settled down by my feet, his favourite bit of me. H is at my bedside by the time I struggle out. God I'm tired...
To his credit, H, bless him, has not balked yet at going back to bed.
Ten minutes later: Bzzz... beep...
Oh for the love of...
Oh wait it's the bleeper showing low battery. It was fully charged when I started this: I guess it's not used to such treatment!
It continues to do a short buzz and beep every 10 minutes or so. I'm afraid the charger is downstairs and my body feels it's twice its weight as I'm settled into my nice, comfy mattress...
Shove it under the pillow...

6.43am

He's here again. The young one I mean, G is still a rather large obstacle in the bottom of my bed. I've been turning this way and that pulling my legs up. Should probably have moved him but didn't want to risk another little night owl demanding my attention... just so tired, and my dodgy shoulder is really aching from lying on it... ow...
The young one announces that "H can get ipad upstairs."
Oh yes all right then... it's close enough to getting up time I suppose... grumble grumble...

Me: "Yes, H can get ipad into Mummy's bedroom now because it's 7 o'clock!"

Well nearly.

H: "See Daddy for 17 minutes... see Daddy at 17 o'clock..."

Oh, I've muddled him again, bum. Never mind, he seems happy.

I know, I know, I'm just going with the flow here!!

This is the period where we still have a bit of a rest in bed before going downstairs.

Right, there's way too much fidgeting, I'm knackered.

"H go to H's room to play with trains please."

Off he goes: peace.

Oh G has got up now and is amusing himself. He's back with a pack of pears he wants me to open; fine.

In the next half hour H comes back 3 more times, each time results in me sending him off to play with his cars or trains.

On one of his trips back to his room he says something to me which really touches me, as the way he says it is new. Trouble is I'm beyond knackered now... must write it down... zzz... Oh... I come awake again as he comes back. I remember what it was, I'm sure he said "I love you Mummy..." or did I dream it?!

7.38am

I finally tell him to take the iPad into his bedroom, off he goes.

Arrgh. He's yelling from his room. What is it H?

"Drink!! No no no no no!!! Mummy in H's bedroom!"

O...kay...

There is of course a drink on the side from the night before. He's a little agitated so I hand it to him.

"H cuddle with Mummy."

I guess he needs a hug after being repeatedly told to sling his hook throughout the night! I put his DVD on yet again and leave.

This buys me a bit more time but it really doesn't feel like long enough... so tired...

Well I'm sure H is not sleeping from the first time he comes in. The DVD buys a bit of time before he comes out again and again. The annoying thing is when he comes into our bed and we let him stay he goes to sleep, not so in his own room.

Later on in the morning H went out with Steve for a Dads and kids activity at the library. He was generally a bit disruptive, not really interested in the activities, running around the place, then crashed out for a kip in the car on the way home. He's only had maybe 15 minutes sleep though, so we'll see what happens tonight.

13th January 2013
Operation Bedtime: Night 2

It's Daddy's turn to do the rapid returns to bed for H, while Mummy sleeps downstairs to catch up after last night.

6am
H goes in. Steve ushers him back and tells him he must stay in H's bed.
That's it.
Seriously, 6am?!
There is just no justice in the world!

He could've just been really zonked from the night before (I know I was!) so Daddy is going to take tonight's shift too, check it's not a fluke!

13th January 2013
Family Sunday

Chasing each other, giggling madly, up and down stairs...
G then plonks himself down on the armchair near where Steve is in the lounge, curls himself into a foetal ball and rocks a little. H climbs up too, curling his arm around G, and lays his cheek down onto G's back.
That's love I guess.

Afternoon Tea
We are in a cafe, G has picked the cake he wanted and has gouged the icing off of it before I've even paid for it – he's a little exuberant today!
H is eating an ice cream.

"Don't want to be sick!!"
Hmm... hope he's not trying to tell me something...

G is being incredibly mischievous, I was attempting to entertain him by blowing bubbles but that didn't last. He darts away from me. No problem, I can catch him up...I just can't lift him as he assumes the "boulder pose" by hunkering down onto the floor in the foetal position. This is surprisingly effective in resisting movement of any kind. My only strategy is to waggle my stiffened fingers through under his arms (not easy!) then hastily link my fingers across his chest, hauling him up and bouncing him back to our table one step at a time.
It really is quite a workout.

8pm
So I've been lounging in the bath with a trashy novel, surrounded by candles, then I've been gazing into my wood fire… and guess what? Night 2 of Op Bedtime was such a piece of piss for Steve he's doing tonight too!! It's like BOGOF for uninterrupted kip!!

The choir girls are still a big part of my "family" – once the kids are in bed I sometimes pop onto Facebook, and there they are; gossiping and having a giggle. A desire to wee and spit out drink with laughter is often mentioned… along with frequent references to people's crushes… just a big bunch of kids really, but I love 'em! The online chats really kept me company on the nights when hubby wasn't here, buoyed me up, helped keep me sane!

14th January 2013
Operation Bedtime: Night 3

Hubby did night 3 for me, as he'd had such an easy time on night 2.
He's just told me that for the last few nights he hasn't been doing the bedtime folder with H, the one that says time for bed, under the duvet etc.
This is what he does instead:
After H has had his story Steve says "H and bear stay in H's bed all night, don't come into Daddy's bed."

Steve then puts the DVD on, saying "H have music."
"He then says "Night night, Daddy turn out the light, Daddy shut the door.""
H repeats all these.

So that's a bit different to what Annie and I do!

Anyway H's first trip in was at 1.10am. Steve said "Not Daddy's bed!" and ushered him back.
Nothing was then heard until 4am when he was chattering to himself, then 4.30 he needed a new nappy, before going back to bed again.

Hmm... could things be settling down a bit?

14th January 2013
Christmas and New Year: in January!

It's snowing outside, H and I are getting in the car to go to school.

H pipes up: "Christmas in January... Father Christmas in January!!"
Oh no... Just because it's snowing…
Me: "Christmas finished!"
Phew, that seemed to have worked!
H: "Snowflakes on your tongue!!"
Oh, go on then!

H has recorded numerous home movies on the ipod. In one of them he is singing, but we can't quite work it out, it's very quiet...
When asked what he's singing, his reply is "H singing shoo-bole song."
At first I thought he was singing "Perfect" by Pink, but the rhythm wasn't right. After more listening I suss it out: what sounds like "perfect time" is actually "Auld Lang Syne!"
Happy New Year – again!!

Despite the snow and freezing-ness outside it's cosy here in our quirky old house. (For quirky read creaky, strangely wired, needs work!) I've finally got the knack of lighting a fire in the wood burner and spend time in front of it sorting paperwork. Today, it's the long overdue Conners questionnaire about H, that is used to assess for ADHD. G has already got those particular letters after his name – clever lad eh?! I'm going to see if we have the matching set...

15th January 2013
Operation Bedtime: Night 4

Hubby took the shift last night again. I know, aren't I lucky!! Something a little different did occur after he put H to bed.
Steve spoke as usual: "H and Teddy stay in H's bed all night, not to go into Daddy's bed."
H repeated this, then unprompted said: "Go to Daddy's bed would be bad!" This was an un-prompted comment I promise you – obviously H's take on being repeatedly told to stay away!

We'll see what happens...

1.30am
Door alarm wasn't activated, but Steve could hear H chatting and laughing in his room so went in to put him back in bed and tell him to go to sleep.

5.30am
Same as above... are we getting there?!

15th January 2013
Snow day

For once Norfolk is in the news, as there are around 260 schools closed due to snow and ice.

7.30am
Spare a thought for us in the snow here...
We've had a meltdown with H in pyjamas in the garden before
breakfast: "BUILD A SNOWMAN!!!"

Ok, ok... cue the foot high pile of ice hastily clumped together with a couple of stick arms shoved in haphazardly...
Couldn't even get dressed or go to the loo: it's quite nippy outside in your dressing gown you know!

Ok it's snowing too much here... although H's school is still open at the moment the driving conditions to get him in are too hazardous. I've already told him that G's school is closed because of too much snow, that G is on holiday. I tell H that he's not going to school today either.

8.30am
Me: "School closed today, too much snow."
H: "Drive later."
Me: "Too slippery to drive."
H: "Drive to holiday!"
Me: "Holiday at home, a day off school is a holiday!"

Well once upon a time that wouldn't have worked!

Later...
Ok the above conversation is being repeated quite a lot so maybe I'm not home free on that one yet...

10.30am
I've togged G up to the eyeballs so he could go out in the garden in the snow.
One minute (and I do mean one minute) later I see he has his gloves off and is eating handfuls of the white stuff.
By the time I go to the other room to get my shoes he has dumped his shoes and is wandering around in his socks.
Have now put wellies on him, let's see how long that lasts...

3pm
Of course since I decided to keep H off school because of the weather the sun came out and the roads are totally clear! Never mind, we have come out to the woods and are having a cuppa in the cafe.

G really doesn't want to stay at the table... has been full of pent up energy all day. He is screwing up his features into an angry grimace.

Steve and G are now locked together, forehead to forehead, G grinding nose to nose, Steve gazing at him eyeball to eyeball.

It's like 2 stags locking horns, the younger buck challenging the old patriarch... who will stare down the other? The challenge slowly morphs into a squeezy hug session... ahh... male bonding...

Hubby is very kindly taking the night time shifts with H while I sleep downstairs away from marauding kids. I guess he does owe me quite a few nights though!

I'm still an insomniac.

I have my own set of rituals:

Tissue for my nose, drink, hot water bottle, kakuro number puzzles, reading book and finally ear plugs then light out. Then sleep.

Maybe.

This is what works for me, eventually.

I've tried most stuff over the years: music, baths, booze... sex.

Yep, that thing that seems to spark most blokes out? It's not happening here.

Every now and then though, maybe every week or two, for a real treat I pop a sleeping tablet.

I probably shouldn't look forward to those nights quite as much as I do...

16th January 2013
Operation Bedtime: Night 5

Midnight

We're still up when I find the young one sat on the stairs. I put him back to bed: "Stay in H's bedroom, don't go into Mummy and Daddy's bed."

1.30am

Steve was upstairs again. The door alarm didn't go, but he heard H try the door handle before moving away again. He was playing, chatting and getting increasingly loud, so Steve went in and put him back to bed again as usual.

4.30am

H comes into Daddy's bedroom but seems very tired. Steve puts him back to bed again. Does he think 4.30am is a good time to get up?? He's not coming out for the 1am slot!

16th January 2013
Feed me... Nah, only kidding!

I'm eating some lamb stew in front of the telly.
(Shock news: I'm a slob given half the chance, you've caught me with a TV dinner.)
G is stood right in front of me (ok can't see the telly now!) and is showing an interest in my plate. Oh ok. I put a bit of lamb on the spoon and hold it out to him. He touches it with his fingers but isn't sure.
I hold it out to him asking if he wants to put the spoon in his mouth, opening my mouth wide to show him.
We spend the next 5 minutes with G opening his mouth wide, leaning towards the spoon but shying away again when it gets within a spoon's width. He's still got his gob open wide though, so looks quite comical as he does this. I'm encouraging him by opening wide too; I guess he thinks I'm comical too as we are soon both giggling away, leaning towards each other, then away, the spoon between us as we gape at each other between chuckles.

16th January 2013
Death by repeating: reprise

H takes AGES to eat his dinner. It's great now he can feed himself (technically!) but he is so slow. He forgets all the time, and needs prompting to take each mouthful.
If he dribbles a bit (always a hazard) I have to clean it up quick. G meanwhile gives us endless requests to open the cupboard for different types of crisps that rarely get wholly eaten. Oops, H has now been at the stew so long it's gone stone cold. I tell him I'll warm it up.
"Warm up the dinner. Warm up Mummy..."
Naturally I have to repeat all of this.
"Eat Mummy... Mummy is not a food... it would hurt Mummy if you eat a food!"
Repeat... gritted teeth...
"Warm up phone game flag!"
More repeating... Guess what's coming...

"Phone game flag is not a food... it would break it phone game flag if it was a food..."
Yes H. Grrr...
"It would break it phone game flag if it was a food!!!"
All right, all right...

Finally he finishes the stew, and hands me the bowl.
"H stand on the tree... it's impossible to stand on the tree... it would break it if you fall!"
Yes, yes... repeat, repeat...groan.

One of H's obsessions is having a set rota of phrases, such as "it's impossible to stand on the tree... H stand on the sky, it's impossible to stand on the sky...
He says this stuff sometimes more, sometimes less, but always several times daily. Sadly part of his obsession is getting me to repeat all this stuff back to him. Precisely, with no variations. Hence my lack of emphasis on correcting his use of language and grammar. I really don't want to add any more words into the mix...

16th January 2013
Translating H-speak

Sometimes I get muddled with what H wants from me speech-wise. First there is the polite request to ask me to repeat after him. 'Polite request' equals saying the same phrase over and over in an increasingly stressy fashion until I say it too. And then there is the time when he actually wants an answer to a question.
Example:
Snow in the swimming pool.
There was a lot of snow which kept H off school, meaning he missed his much loved swimming lesson.
He obviously wanted me to repeat this, ok.

H: "Pool is on."
Me: "Pool is on."
H: "Pool is on!"
Me: "Pool is on!!"
H: "Pool is on!!!"
Me: "Pool is on...?"

Oh, hold on a minute... he's asking me when the next swimming session is!

For goodness sake... need an interpreter...

Now he is playing under a blanket.

H: "Blanket is...?"

I don't know, what is it...?

H: "Blanket is...??"

Me: "Blanket is blue?" Well, it is.

H: "Water on the blanket!"

Oh, ok, water is usually shown as blue, therefore...?

And before you ask, no actual water was anywhere in the vicinity of the blanket.

16th January 2013
Have you got worms boy?!

Well as I was saying H takes soooo long to eat his dinner, with constant prompting. Don't they say it's better to eat slowly so your brain realises your stomach's full and you don't overeat? Not here!

After his dinner he has crisps, plus whatever snacks he can minesweep from G's plate. Then yogurt fruit sweets... the requests go on. I have to keep telling him "too much food will make you sick!" His dinner, snack and supper all seem to roll into one. If I didn't know better I'd think he had worms – but he's in nappies remember, and I haven't spotted any evidence of that yet...

17th January 2013
Disappearing act

Probably should get a tracker on G in this big old house... just searched every nook and cranny twice over before finding him kneeling in silence on the window sill behind the curtains upstairs, looking out at the snow...

17ᵗʰ January 2013
Operation Bedtime: Night 6

H was staying in his room before for the midnight / 1am waking, however he's gone back to going into our bedroom.
He was on a roll last night, coming out every hour from around midnight.
Sadly Steve was so knackered that by the time the 5am trip came around he didn't hear the door alarm and slept right through, waking later to find H snoozing next to him... arrgh!!

17ᵗʰ January 2013
Tiredness, repeating and general puppeteering

Due to H being in crazy puppetmaster mode, this morning I have mostly been:
In and out of rooms
Up and down stairs
Had my fingers used to press the ipad.
Daddy has also had to use his fingers on the ipad.

I've had to take Bear out of the house and back into the house, before putting H into the car. Then Daddy had to take Bear to the car, before going back into the house again with Bear.
Wanting me to stop the car, wanting to stay home... the list goes on.

It's really difficult, because with the slow process time it's like he backs up everything that's been said, and needs that extra time. But at the same time it is H that is pushing and pushing us on to repeat the next thing.
For example: we've told him "Bear not in the car" yet he obviously wanted the bear in the car, and will yell this over and over, ever more stressed, trying to get you to repeat it. So when you do, he'll want the bear in the car, but then has to go back to take the bear out of the car again, as that was what was originally said. There's like a delay on everything. No matter how long we originally pause to allow him to process, it's like the stress he's in doesn't allow him to process that time anyway. He's always on the back foot. Hence the desperate

puppeteering and constant instructions... maybe he's trying to catch up, before the final understanding can get through. Does that make any sense?? I know, sometimes I don't know whether I'm coming or going!

Had another insomniac session last night: yep, I know it's my own bloody stupid fault, you don't need to tell me! I'm feeling a little bit tired and weepy after H's really, really controlling behaviour this morning. He's even displayed this at school for the first time really.

After getting out of the car I made the rookie mistake of taking one glove off in the car and leaving one on, as I have terrible circulation and my fingers go numb in the cold. Well we went inside and H immediately started: "H gloves on, H gloves on....!!"
Me: "We're inside, H doesn't need gloves on, we have gloves on outside!"
I quickly took my one remaining glove off, but he wasn't having any of it. I managed to get him to the classroom, H all the way keeping up his mantra of "gloves on." Usually he changes his behaviour at school, but I guess he was sufficiently tired and fretty to carry it on. His TA tried to explain about the gloves off inside thing, showing him her gloves in her bag waiting for break time, but it was no good. He struggled to get them on himself, at which point of course we could take them off again: and... re-set.

Anyway, I'd arranged to meet a friend for coffee, I was going to be about half an hour late, but that was ok... still just feel that we've taken a small step back again, as I'm finding myself emotionally affected by it all.
Still, I drove off to meet my friend, looking forward to chai latte and cake in this minus 8 degree morning, yelling: "Don't cry, you knob!!"at myself – which seemed to work, just. Bonus!

18th January 2013
Op Bedtime: Night 7

Last night there were a couple of times H stayed playing in his room, until the noise got such that Steve had to put him back to bed. After that he came into our bedroom again a couple of times. Interestingly though, he is not getting into our bed any more, just standing by the side of the bed.

H knows the drill now – he often prompts Steve to say "don't come into Mummy and Daddy's bed."

We really need to change the wording to "Don't come into Mummy and Daddy's bedroom." Though we do say stay in H's bedroom, it might be worth a try!

H is at respite for the next 2 nights so we'll see how it goes when he's back.

19th January 2013
Child free!!

G has gone to respite tonight now too. It feels like it's been a long time coming, this night where both boys are away at the same time. It'll be quite a novelty to kip in the marital bed with hubby tonight!

So we have been in a coffee shop for 2 hours now, just hubby and me.

Why?

Because we can!!

20th January 2013
Mealtimes

With prompting on every bite, each the size of a mousy nibble, it's only taken H an hour and 35 minutes to eat a bread roll, 3 inches of celery and 5 tiny pieces of pepper. Needless to say I spooned the yogurt down his neck myself...

20th January 2013
At the playbarn

H is eating an ice cream, as always this is his treat at the playbarn. He is wearing lined trousers, we notice a small rip in the outer layer. Hmm...

"New nappy?"

Ok, can we eat the ice cream first...?
Nope. He's being a bit slow with the ice cream and is starting to ask over and over...
"No eat ice cream first then nappy!"
Ok, ok...
H carry ice cream new nappy..."
Mmm... hygienic!
Mummy and Daddy get H new nappy baby changing!!"

Escalating fast now, ok both of us have to go into the disabled loo with him. (It's ok, a friend is keeping an eye on G!) There is a baby changing table in there, we have the conversation most times as to how H is "too big for the baby changing."
Oh well, we are all in the loo, H is lying on the floor, dribbling ice cream in hand. I decide to help the ice cream situation by promptly eating half of it. You've got to take the benefits where you can...
Steve meanwhile is attending to the business end, when H perks up: "Bum up!" This isn't actually anything we've said... but I do remember his assistant from nursery 4ish years ago telling me she had said that once, and he had gleefully repeated it... but he must have heard it since then; surely he's not remembering from then, that would be silly... or would it...?

"H eating bum up... dobbling, dobbling, dobbling pop!"
What?!? Situation normal on the language side of things then!
20 minutes later we have to repeat the whole performance. We even had increasingly stressy requests for ice cream but we managed to fob him off with that one.
We're in the loo again...
"New trousers!!"
Oh... ok... haven't got any spares...
I smuggle them behind my back and turn them inside out so the rip doesn't show... ta-da!!

Crisis averted.

20th January 2013
Op Bedtime: phase 2

H is back from respite and I've put him to bed tonight, with no bedtime folder, the same way hubby does it. I have made the addition of saying: "Don't come into Mummy and Daddy's bedroom" with H tagging on the end "all night!!"

21st January 2013
Balanced diet

You know when you buy your child a present and they just play with the packaging? We've kind of got a similar thing going on here where we buy mini Babybel cheeses and G just tries to eat the wax.
Hey ho.

22nd January 2013
H's home movies

One of H's latest crazes is to video himself singing and chatting on my phone, then to play it back endlessly. Over about a week he had put about 80 snippets on there. I'm going through some of them when H comes to listen...

"Head, shoulders, knees and toes… and your chin, and your tongue, and your private, and your belly button, and your eyebrows, and your oin..."

Me: "Where's your oin?! H point to Mummy's oin."
He points to the area of my tummy.
Me: "That's my tummy!"
H: "I don't know where's your oin... I don't know means where's your oin..."

Oh well at least that's 2 of us that don't know what it is!

24th January 2013
Sleeping through the night!!

After changing from the DVD at night (lots of visits during the night, turning disk on again, probably no sleep) to music disks at night (couple of visits during the night turning on disk again) we have gone to having the radio on really low – and guess what? It worked!!

I know what you're going to say, it's not rocket science is it; he's waking when the disk/music stops? But trust me, we have gone down the radio route before and it made no difference. So maybe a change is as good as a rest and all that, but I'm cautiously optimistic... let's hope it wasn't just a one-off!

25th January 2013
Can I at least go for a pee?!

Well H is in full flow, forced parroting and puppeteering mode. We are being hustled from pillar to post in an attempt to forestall meltdown, while he teeters on the brink.

Don't you just love speed waddling out of the toilet, hoisting your knickers up from around your ankles to the dulcet strains of "MUMMY IN THE DINING ROOM!!!"

26th January 2013
H speak

"15 toes!"

Cheeky monkey, not only are my fingers "claws" – now I've got 15 toes too. I think he's trying to turn me into the Gruffalo!

30th January 2013
Odds and evens

I'm getting a lot of chatter lately about Mummy being an odd and Daddy being an even...

Today: "One odd old home (our old house) Two even new house home."
Huh?!

31st January 2013
Getting a cold

H has been quite sniffly the last couple of days but he seems more full of cold this evening. He's been happy enough though... He's now sat at the table eating toast and a few crisps.

H was laughing looking at videos he's done on my phone, when he made it vibrate somehow.
The next 10 minutes were spent with me repeating after him back to back "H's at failed" and being gripped around the neck while he cries.
Eventually we are able to wipe his eyes a few times, him prompting me "don't be crying!"
Well you can never quite second guess everything...

A few minutes later again he wants me to repeat endlessly "H sit at the table..."
I'm losing the plot... I decide to ignore it: NOT the right answer!!
He is escalating fast again... bugger, bugger...
I end up shouting the words he wants to hear very loudly and slowly...
Surprisingly, that doesn't make him happy: I wonder why Mother!

"Sick in the bag."
Uh oh. He remembers the sick bags when we went on the ferry.
I get a bowl which he accepts instead, but doesn't do anything.
He is gripping me again, then getting me to move his bear, plate, and crisp bag minutely from place to place.
All his anxiety is highlighted as he says sick in the bowl, then no sick in the bowl in between me moving the things around.

Bless him... could be man flu...

1st February 2013
Need the patience of a saint – except sadly I'm not a saint...

H is still on what I call "high alert" for his mood.

He is sat at the table with Bear on the table to his left and ipad on the table to his right as always.

"H's at table."

Me: "Yes, H's at table." (I've said it before, correcting speech or grammar doesn't come into this, I've tried!)

"H's at table!!"

Crap.

I lost count of how many times I kept repeating "H's at table" after him during the next 5 or 10 minutes as it was like a quick volley tennis match, but it was probably around the 80 mark. All the time keeping my tone of voice quite calm, while his escalated into frenzied crying and screaming. That probably doesn't sound too stressful.

Trust me, it was.

"H's at table... H's at table... *H's at table!!* H's at table... *H's at TABLE!!!* H's at...*" well, you get the idea.

When I'd hit the 80 odd mark I had one of my marvellous Mummy moments, and just screamed at the top of my lungs, sucking in a huge breath before each word: "H'S... AT... TABLE!!!!!"

My throat actually hurt.

Of course the angry, stressed crying, turned to upset, looking for comfort crying. I was then able to cuddle him to get him to calm down, breaking the awful cycle of being stuck in repeat mode. So I guess at least *something* good came out of my own little meltdown.

2nd February 2013
Eagle eye H

After H reads a 5mm high character on the computer from his seat 10 feet behind me I tell him he's got "eagle eyes."

"H got eagle eyes!"

He wanders off, peers closely at himself in the mirror, then calmly sits back down to resume his breakfast.

He must have a distorted image of the features of an eagle now, along with the ears of a bat...

3rd February 2013
Yes I have started that diet thank you...

"Charlotte is a one girl... Mummy is a 15 girls!"
I'm hoping this is a language muddle... and not that H thinks I'm 15 times the size of Charlotte, whoever she may be.

4th February 2013
Training up a deputy

So H has smacked G who is hanging around the locked back door, as you are not allowed to keep trying the door handle unless you are *actually* going out. (H's rules not mine!) Well hubby tells him off, and of course H can't cope and goes into meltdown. G absconds upstairs quick smart to escape the racket.

H is now trying to start his calming ritual. Can vary slightly with words and stuff, but generally meltdown and calming ritual goes like this:
H will leap around the room slamming down onto his knees, bang his wrists or the backs of his hands on the carpet – hard.
Then he'll say a lot of different stuff like "hurt your hand / head / knee" in order for you to repeat it. This has to be done correctly, you mustn't change the words around! Also repeat any noises that he makes exactly. Then you have to cuddle him (his death grip around your neck) and wipe his eyes, saying all of this after him.
So that's that.

Here's the thing: Daddy told him off, so Daddy has to make good on the calming ritual.

H is not calming down though, as although Daddy is wandering around saying "Hurt your hand H" or whatever, he is putting some tools away or something. I mean, now is not the time to start multi-tasking!

H is in full pelt, screaming and throwing himself around, between following Daddy around yelling things up at him to repeat.

I tell Steve H needs his full attention; Steve telling him off was the catalyst for the meltdown, so Steve needs to be the one to fix it. Moreover he needs to drop what he's doing and just give H his full attention, as the meltdown worsens really quickly.

Me: "It's his ritual!"

Steve: "It's fucking pathetic!!" He is pretty stressed by this time, understandably.

Great, good thing H is too stressed to start playing with that language!

Me: "No, it's his autism!!"

Most of the time I've been writing, Steve has been a weekend Daddy / husband. Now he's home we are entering a different phase... I know of couples that have split up, in part due to the stress of parenting children with different needs, challenging behaviours. To be honest there was a moment a few years back, just before I started writing, when I thought it could happen to us. We are lucky; we have a strong marriage. When you have a strong partnership you are better able to deal with life when it shits on you. But when life shits on you and you also belatedly realise you have 2 little people that will rely on you heavily, for life; that you are always going to be their everything, it's terrifying. Certainly for me, as I said in the prologue, they are my joy, my loves, but also the worry that I won't always be able to be their rock, mentor, carer, assistant, is there when you dare to think about it.

So that's why we don't think about it too much: and when I do, I know I have a loving partner and friends that will be my rock, who are in the same boat as me; or quite simply care about me, as I do about them.

I'll never tell anyone what to do; you've read the book, I've done stuff through trial and error, and sometimes sheer gut instinct. Hopefully I haven't scarred the poor boys for life!!

But one thing I will say is, seek out support from your friends when you need it —
they care about you.
And for God's sake keep a sense of humour!!

Obviously the story of our family is an evolving one, the transition to
adulthood – oh boy that's going to be interesting!!
I guess it would be easier on society if we could get our 2 autistic lads
to fit into the neurotypical world. It's been a struggle over the years,
things that happened even before this diary started.

The grinding exhaustion, the struggle to get help with respite for
which I'm forever grateful to have received. The sheer physical
sickness I felt when G bolted and I had all my friends out looking for
him, the crashing relief on finally spying him settling down to sleep in
the twilight on the local play equipment.
The headbutting and high-pitched screaming phase that G went
through, when he had a permanent bald patch rubbed away on the
centre of his forehead.

I've felt depression, anxiety, anger, despair. I was in a kind of
alternate universe for a while there, for the first few years I was
adjusting to the sleep deprivation.

I still feel anxiety and upset at times, of course I do. Don't all
parents? And way, way too tired most of the time. But I also feel
contented more often now, endlessly intrigued, often bemused and
sometimes laugh out loud happy.

A sense of humour definitely helps. You need one of those.

I remember when G started smearing.
The first time we took our eye off the ball while dealing with infant
H I was called upstairs by an angry husband. We were both really
tired: what's new?! I went into G's room to find a naked G, faeces
smeared on every visible surface including himself. You wouldn't
think his little body would contain that much... my hubby was rather

affronted when I laughed out loud! Never mind, I said, you run the bath, I'll get the industrial strength carpet cleaner...

What actually helped me was learning, striving to understand what makes my boys tick. For me, rather than trying to get them to fit into 'our' world, I did my best to see into their minds so that I could fit into theirs.

Now, I hope, we are learning to meet each other half way; I don't know if this is what society wants, but it is what our family needs. I feel that everyone that gets to know our boys is better off for it, in gaining a greater understanding and empathy for their fellow human beings, of whatever ability. Well I hope so anyway; and I know, I would say that - they're my sons!
They are simply wired differently, and have as great a capacity for love as any neurotypical child I have known.

Surviving as a happy family unit would not, could NOT, have happened without the help of a lot of people:
The good friends I have made through the local support group and also in the community where I lived for so many years.
Our family, who though far away have helped us where they can: particularly in giving us that bit of respite that made a trip simply staying away from home and being sleepless somewhere else, into a holiday.
All the good friends that have touched our lives, taking our lads at face value, and coming to love them for the fascinating young people they are.

My 2 lads are classed as having autism with a severe learning disability, which means we can access the social services children with disabilities team. I am actually very lucky in this: sadly a lot of my friends aren't able to access the services that this opens up, and struggle in vain for the respite and occupational therapy that has made our lives so much easier to cope with.

I seriously think I would have gone insane without
A: the fabulous people who provide overnight respite and

B: help from the various personal assistants employed through the direct payments system.

These wonderful people who have become good friends certainly don't do it for the money – there must be much easier ways of making a few quid!

I'm aware that our family is reliant on the government for this help, and I dread any cuts that would take away such hard won respite. (Trust me, that's another story!)

I still don't think too far ahead. Living for now is challenging enough, but hopefully we're getting there. I hope that maybe society can try to understand people like my lads. Everyone involved with someone on the spectrum has a different story to tell, as do people on the spectrum themselves; I just wanted to share some tales of "G Force" and "H Bomb" with you.

Thanks for listening.

ABOUT THE AUTHOR

You want to know about the author?
Really, haven't you heard enough?!

Ok.

The author lives in Norfolk with her hubby and 2 boys, trying to be
the best wife and mother she can within her limited means.
When sufficiently awake she loves to read in the bath, draw by the
sea, potter in the garden, visit her friends.
Oh and cake is always nice. And Chinese takeaway.

Most of all she loves hugging her sons when they want to hug her.
Yep, that's kind of addictive.

8979096R00154

Printed in Great Britain
by Amazon.co.uk, Ltd.,
Marston Gate.